Arthur Adams

Travels of a naturalist in Japan and Manchuria

Arthur Adams

Travels of a naturalist in Japan and Manchuria

ISBN/EAN: 9783741182754

Manufactured in Europe, USA, Canada, Australia, Japa

Cover: Foto ©Andreas Hilbeck / pixelio.de

Manufactured and distributed by brebook publishing software (www.brebook.com)

Arthur Adams

Travels of a naturalist in Japan and Manchuria

MANCHU WOMAN.

TRAVELS OF A NATURALIST
IN
JAPAN AND MANCHURIA.

THE MUSINA.
Native of Japan.

BY

ARTHUR ADAMS, F.L.S.
STAFF-SURGEON, R.N.

CONTENTS.

CHAPTER I.

Land's End to Rio Janeiro—Life on the Ocean—Natural Phenomena—Inhabitants of the High Seas—Incidents and Reflections—Land in Sight—Rio Janeiro—City of San Sebastian 1

CHAPTER II.

Land-Crabs and Tiger-Beetles—Inhabitants of an Aloe—Ferns and Flowers—Insects attracted by a Lighthouse—A Useful Aloe—Rockwork—Natural Aquariums—Crabs at Dinner—The Hidden Waters—A Negro Market—The Gold Bug 18

CHAPTER III.

The Cape of Good Hope—A Four Days' Beetle Hunt—Millar's Point—Whales' Bones—Fish "galore"—Wrecked Violet-Snails—A Stranded Fiddle-fish—Cormorants and Penguins—Burrowing-Snails—A Vegetable Parachute . . 30

CHAPTER IV.

PAGE

The Gate of the East—Under the Fig Tree—Javanese Market
—Monkeys for Sale—Jungle Scene—"Massacre of the
Innocents"—Centipedes and Scorpions—The Tiger's Paw
—A Ludicrous Incident—New Island—Description of a
Coral Reef—Gutta-percha Trees—A Deserted Village—
Hornbills : 42

CHAPTER V.

A Visit to the Pratas Shoal—The Padi Bird—A Desolate Island
—The Joss-House—Lilliputian Forest—Gannets—Rock-
Basins—Odd Fishes—Musical Fishes—Ancient Quarries
—Banks of the Tchu-kiang 56

CHAPTER VI.

An Apology for Beetles—Village Trees—The Buffalo and the
Fanqui—Danes Island—Boy Hunters—Habits of Ants—
Flowers compared with those of England—North and
South, a Porcine Contrast—Reservoirs in Canton—
Monster Aquarium—Pond Shell-fish—The Scaly Ant-
eater—Master Wouff and "Scales" 69

CHAPTER VII.

Stroll through Villages on the Yang-tsze-Kiang—Spring-time
—The Pupa Gatherer—How to fatten Ducks—Charac-
teristic Scene—Banks of the Great River—Freshwater
Crabs—Eriocheir Japonicus—Youthful Poachers—The
Mina Bird—Adventures of a Thousand-legs . . . 84

CHAPTER VIII.

Miatau Islands—Probable Origin of some Stories about Sea-serpents—Alceste Island—Seals—Fishing Cormorant—The Blue Rock-pigeon—Kala-hai—A Fishing Party—Bustards—Snake-like Fishes—Gulf of Pecheli—Strange-looking Craft—Native Fishermen—A Shower of Beetles—The Black Surf-Duck 97

CHAPTER IX.

The Great Wall—Quaint-looking Watch-house—Inquisitive Sons of Ham—Visit to the Temples—Birds Shot by our Sportsmen—Hawking at the Great Wall—Flowers and Insects—Wreck of the Medusa—Scarcity of Land Shells—Humming-bird Hawk-moth—The Shield Shrimp—Staunton Island 110

CHAPTER X.

The Korea—Among the Islands—Odd Names of Mountain Peaks—Victoria Harbour—Beacon Fires—Visit from the Natives—Their Picturesque Appearance—Description of the Chief—Costume of the Natives—Worship of Bacchus—Their Rude Manners—Their Curiosity—Modes of Salutation—An Anecdote 125

CHAPTER XI.

Exciting Incident—Korean Tombs—Mode of Burial—Dwellings in the Korea—Japanese Outpost—An Entertainment—Hamel's "Travels"—Language of the Koreans—A Commendable Custom—Religious Belief—Priests and Nuns 138

CHAPTER XII.

Port of Mah-lu-san—A Seining Party—Beautiful Scene—Hauling the Seine—A Viviparous Fish—Encounter with a Snake—A Clever Thief—Deer Island—Buck Shooting—Lichens and Toads—The Sunny Gorge—Wilford's Rest—Range of the Tiger 153

CHAPTER XIII.

Russian Manchuria—The Coast Line—The Conquerors of China—Tartar Bravery—Province of Liao-tung—Dangerous Navigation—Mouth of the Liao-ho—A Land of Pigs—Use of Cotton Seeds—Furriers' Shops—Food Plants of Manchuria—Chinese Influence—Dagelet Island—Sea Bears—Bay of Sio-wu-hu—Manchurian Bulls—The Manchus 167

CHAPTER XIV.

Wild Cattle—The Dog and his Master—A Haul of Salmon—Seaweed-collecting Fishermen—A Jovial Crew—A Weakness for Skulls—Olga Bay—Capture of a Strange Insect—Place of Refuge for Old Seals—Appearance of three Ainos—St. Vladimir Bay—A Useful Beacon—The Emerald Wing 185

CHAPTER XV.

Expedition to an Inland Lake—Search for New Specimens—Change of Scene—Botanical Observations—Orthopterous Insects—Dragon-flies—Trapa natans—"Dash" discomfited—A Picnic Party—Capture of Crustaceans for Dinner—Enthusiastic Beetle-hunters—Charred and Blackened Trees—Cryptochiton Stelleri—An Impressive Scene . 204

CHAPTER XVI.

Risiri—Effects of a Violent Gale—Rifunsiri Island—Deserted Fishing Sheds—Todomisiri or Seal Island—Aniwa Bay—The Duck Family in Full Feather—Ornithology of the Island—Abodes of the Ainos—A Domestic Scene—Dress of the Men—Feminine Ornament—The Hairy Kuriles . 222

CHAPTER XVII.

Hakodadi—Vegetation—Pleasing Aspect of the Scenery—Appearance of the Town—A Temple of Budha—Visit to the Theatre—The Audience and the Play—Vicinity of the Town—A Charming Retreat—Intercourse with Nature 241

CHAPTER XVIII.

Beautiful Tsu-Sima—Mussel Cove and Oyster Sound—The Adela Moth—Paulownia Imperialis—Fossil Trees—Capture of a Damaster—Gigantic Oysters—Island of Sado—Shooting Party—Fortune's Beetle—Diard's Pheasant—Nisi Bama—Beautiful Spectacle—Squid Fishing—Squid Village—Taxus Fruit—An Odd Fish . . . 253

CHAPTER XIX.

Nagasaki—The Scenery—Vegetation—Insect Life—Lacquer Trees—The Woodcutter—The Harbour—Desima and Pappenberg—State Barge and Pleasure Boats—Scenes in the Streets—Mendicant Priest—A Bonze—Strolling Acrobats—Cemeteries—Ceremonies in Honour of the Dead—The Temples—Dog-Fancier's Shop—Gigantic Salamanders—Fish Festival—A Ramble in Kiusiu . . 267

CHAPTER XX.

The Seto-Uchi, or Inland Sea—Tomo—Gay Spectacle—The Temple—Tea-house in the Suburb—Priest and Dancing Girls—Women of Japan—The Niphon Belle at Home—Female Costume—Unbecoming Fashions—House of a Wealthy Native of Tomo—Saki Distilleries—Yokohama—Curiosity-Shops—Beautiful Carved Work—Japanese Contrasts—Naruto or Whirlpool 284

CHAPTER XXI.

Simidsu Excursionists—Quack Doctors—Natural Curiosities—Habits of the Musina—Ursa Major and Minor—Women hauling the Seine—Waterfalls at Fat-si-jou—Singular Caddis Worms—Prolific Life—Village Store—Mode of catching Whales—Japanese Mammals—Madrepores and Mollusca—Shell Sand—Araki—Sun-and-Moon Shell . 302

CHAPTER XXII.

The Literature of Japan—Books—Illustrations—Voyage Home—Oceanic Phenomena—Black Fish—Bonitoes—Dolphins—Floating Tree—Pelagian Molluscs—Sea Nettles—Skeleton Shrimps—Sailor Crabs—Rapid Growth of Barnacles—A Pretty Kettle of Fish 323

TRAVELS OF A NATURALIST

IN

JAPAN AND MANCHURIA.

CHAPTER I.

Land's End to Rio Janeiro—Life on the Ocean—Natural Phenomena—Inhabitants of the High Seas—Incidents and Reflections—Land in Sight—Rio Janeiro—City of San Sebastian.

EARLY in the year we left England in H.M. ship "Actæon," bound for Rio Janeiro, our object being to survey the little islands at the entrance of the glorious harbour. On the passage from the Land's End to Madeira we had beautiful weather. A few days previously a gale had swept along the coast, and though there was a heavy swell the surface of the sea was smooth. We were amused, on reaching a warmer latitude than that which we had left, at watching the pretty bright guillemots which floated on the surface, or dived beneath the waves. We observed, also, with interest, the movements of a few divers which were disporting themselves about the ship. We occasionally diverted the monotony of the voyage by fishing for grey gurnards, several of which we captured with a hook and line astern. This novel sport was both exciting and successful.

As we approached the anchorage off Funchal a few flying-fish were seen springing from the water, although, as a rule, they are seldom met with before the tropics are reached. They become more and more numerous as we approach the Equator; and familiar as is the sight of these beautiful creatures to all who traverse the ocean, their flight is invariably watched with interest.

From the time of Columbus, Magellan, De Gama, and other "Argonauts of the fifteenth and sixteenth centuries," to the present day, when the splendid steamers of the Cunard and Inman lines cross the broad bosom of the Atlantic, and "think nothing of it," the same incidents have occurred, and the same ocean phenomena have been observed. This must be my apology for mentioning the inevitable flying-fish. When, as not unfrequently happens, the poor creature flies on board exhausted, it is picked up from the deck, and the "clever one" who secures the prize, holds it in his hand and delivers a profound discourse on its habits and peculiarities to the listening crew. It may not be generally known that besides the common flying-fish, which is very similar to a herring, there are other winged denizens of the deep. The flying-gurnard, for instance, takes its flight from the surface of the ocean, and the little Pegasus, or flying-horse, may frequently be seen rising from the water.

The appearance of the dolphin is always watched for with eager curiosity. We saw many of the long-nosed species as they passed the ship. This is not the sailor's dolphin, which is like a mackerel with a straight forehead, and which changes its colours when dying, but the true delphinus of the ancients, upon whose back rode the musical Arion. The better known and even familiar porpoises were a never-failing fund of amusement, as they raced with the vessel, or gambolled in the foam which she cast up about her bows. The sudden appearance of the little petrels, which, under the name of Mother Carey's chickens, are so dear to seamen, though their presence is regarded as the herald of a storm, was another source of interest. The observation of these and other natural phenomena afforded an inexhaustible fund of amusement as the favourable breeze bore us joyfully on our way. Then, as sometimes happened, our progress was impeded by a calm, when a boat was lowered for the purpose of picking up violet-snails, or capturing a "vessel" from the fleet of "Portuguese-men-of-war."

When evening drew on apace we had other ways of passing the time. "All hands" were invited by the boatswain's pipe to dance and skylark. Sailors are proverbially merry and light-hearted, and the hornpipe and the reel were kept up with unflagging spirit. Those who could sing favoured their comrades with a song; the witty were always ready with the merry gibe, while the scraping of the fiddle and the "basting of the bear" were sources of amusement to others. The officers played at leap-frog or duck-stone on the quarter-deck, or wiled away the time in reading, chess, or cards. The amateur musician brought forth melancholy notes from his beloved flute, and the contemplative man lay supine upon the deck and gazed upon the stars. The heavens, indeed, were now specially worthy of regard, for we had crossed the line, and another hemisphere, with other constellations, was now disclosing itself to our view.

The Southern Cross and Magellanic clouds had taken the place of the North star. Our old stellar friends were lost to view, and the sight of many constellations and new stars was a constant source of interest. Nor must I fail to mention that at this point of our voyage the usual absurd and noisy ceremonies in honour of Neptune were not forgotten.

The ocean, in these low latitudes, presents several phenomena which are particularly interesting to the naturalist, and so beautiful that they are regarded with pleasure even by unscientific observers. The forms of life which may be drawn up from the depths of the sea are infinitely varied. At night countless luminous creatures were seen glinting and sparkling in its black depths. Nothing can be conceived more capricious than their vagaries as they dart hither and thither. To the inquirer into the more recondite secrets of nature these phosphorescent creatures are no less interesting than are the grander luminaries above to the astronomer. The sea-faring man, however, naturally regards with more reverence the moon, the stars, the constellations of the firmament above, as these are his silent companions in his midnight watches, and form his guides across the trackless wastes of ocean.

We were now in the region of the trade winds, of which we took advantage. A steady breeze always filled our sails, which hardly ever required to be trimmed. Our noble vessel, under the influence of the favouring breeze, made rapid progress, and we were all in the best of spirits. How could it be otherwise? The atmosphere was pure and balmy, the sea bright and rippling, the sky flecked with fleecy clouds, and the temperature as genial as could be desired.

During the voyage many events took place which, though trivial in themselves, assumed an air of importance to the "outward bound," and contributed to render our long voyage less tedious and monotonous. One day we spoke a ship and sent letters to our friends at home; the next, perhaps, we fell in with a barnacle-covered fragment of wreck—the sad memento, doubtless, of some tale of suffering and disaster. Haply some sailor on the bowsprit, expert in the use of the "graines," which is a kind of harpoon, kept handy for this especial purpose, impaled occasionally a dolphin or bonito. A huge whale spouting in the distance, the vapour from his blow-holes curling over his head, was an object of intense regard; but the appearance of a school of "black-fish" was hailed with even greater interest. On came these monsters of the deep, dark dusky forms leaping, and rolling, and plunging, following the leader in a long straight line as if they were enjoying themselves to their heart's content. With all these sources of interest and amusement, however, there was much time for meditation and reflection; and we could not help thinking how different were the interests that sway the minds of those "that go down to the sea in ships, and occupy their business in great waters."

An emigrant ship with youth, health, and hope on board goes scudding past, and borne on the breeze comes ever and anon the refrain of their favourite song :—

"To the West! to the West! the Land of the Free!
Where the mighty Missouri rolls down to the sea."

The skipper of an Indiaman, or Ocean Clipper, is thinking only what a splendid passage he will make; the electrician is anxious for the perfection of his tests and the integrity of his cable; the mail agent has eyes only for his letter bags; the sportsman will try his skill upon some unoffending sea-bird; the naturalist explores the bottom for protoplasms, diatomes, and rhizopodes, or skims the surface with his towing-net.

When traversing the great oceans, besides keeping the towing-net always going whenever the ship is not sailing too fast, and whenever the weather is favourable, I always note down on a track-chart every species of bird, fish, or mollusk, I happen to see. If all naturalists did this on their voyage our knowledge of the geographical distribution of marine life would be greatly extended and improved.

In course of time the voyage, which had become somewhat monotonous and even tedious, came to an end, and we all felt the interest excited by the expectation of the first sight of land. Our approach to it was indicated by the appearance of fragile-looking fishing-rafts; by currents having a tendency to take us out of our course; by the colour of the sea, which began to assume a greenish hue; and by floating trees and plants, which, detached from their native soil, were carried towards us.

We gazed long and eagerly for the first view of land, and our patience was rewarded at length by the sight of the famous headland named Cape Frio looming from the distant horizon, a dim undulating line with clouds resting on it. Passing this bare inhospitable promontory, we were soon in sight of the high rocky and irregular coast which forms the safe and wide anchorage of Rio.

The famous harbour of Rio Janeiro presents a view of unparalleled beauty. The scenery around it, indeed, is said to be the most magnificent in the world. As at the decline of day, we sailed under a cloud of canvas, with the wind blowing softly behind, the impression produced on my mind—as it must be on the mind of everyone endowed with a perception of the beautiful in nature—was that of a scene of enchantment.

Rio Janeiro—so named by its discoverer De Sausa—is a misnomer; for, though a number of small rivers flow into the bay from the Organ Mountains, what is called Rio harbour is in reality a noble land-locked bay.

ASCENT OF THE SUGAR-LOAF.

As we approached our destination we passed several uninhabited islets, situated from two to six miles from the entrance of the bay. These appear to be small portions of the rocky mainland detached from it in the infancy of the world. They are now known as Round Island, Flat Island, &c., according to their shape. The entrance to the bay is somewhat narrow, and its western side appears to be guarded by the conical leaning mass of the Sugar-Loaf, while a rocky point of land, on which the fort of Santa Cruz is placed, protects the eastern side. The Sugar-Loaf Rock, which is an enormous cone of solid granite seven hundred feet high, rises abruptly from the sea and has been the scene of several exciting adventures, almost as famous as those of the celebrated Peter Botte mountain in the Mauritius.

An acquaintance of mine, a mere youngster, gave me an account of his own perilous ascent of the Sugar-Loaf, which I will endeavour to render in his own words.

"You know, doctor," he said, "some fellow had planted a flag on the top which had remained there no end of time, so I wasn't going to be beaten by him. So, one fine morning I put some biscuit in my pocket, and my pipe, and started for the top to plant another flag by the side of it; and I scrambled up to a place where the water tumbles over a small rocky chasm, where I had a jolly drink, and put my head under the spout, you know; and when I thought I was almost at the top I found, when I could see anything for the trees, that I was only near the base of the thundering great peak. On I went, however, up the sloping side; and precious hot I can tell you it was. When I got near the top I had very hard work, and tore my clothes, and scratched my knees, and when alongside that confounded fellow's flag, I nearly fainted, and lay down all of a heap.

"It was horrid damp, and I felt a sort of all-over-ishness, as if I was going off the hooks. But I said to myself, 'Never say die,' and began to crawl down again, but I found the rock much steeper than I thought, and slipped and tumbled about like anything. At last," he said, "I gave it up, and began to doze, and feel awfully cold. And so I remained on the top of the blessed mountain ever so long, till I heard, early in the morning, some one shouting, and, creeping near the edge of a big rock, I looked over and saw the gunner and two marines, who were sent by the first lieutenant to look after me. When they saw me up above in such a woeful plight they sang out, 'All right, keep up your spirits,' and that, you know, cheered me up, and I went to meet them almost tumbling down rock after rock; and then, you know, they gave me a drink of rum and water; and—that's all."

Rising from the circumference of the splendid bay, which we now entered, are several rugged mountain peaks, to which have been given fanciful names according to the objects which they are supposed to resemble. Thus, the Paõ de Assuccar, or Sugar-Loaf; the Two Brothers, or Dous Irmaõs; the Parrot's Beak, or the Corcovado, which rears aloft its mighty head more than two thousand feet above the level of the sea. These lofty hills, so varied in colour and outline, are densely wooded, but the different trees which clothe their sides with verdure are undistinguishable in the distance, and only serve to lend a beauty to their bases, while fleecy clouds are sailing round their summits tinged here and there with the hues of the setting sun.

As we drew near to our place of anchorage, boats laden with oranges came out to meet us, and as they approached near the ship were regarded with interest by many a longing eye. The first person who came on board, and greeted us on our arrival, was the officer of health, a rather self-important looking personage; and soon after him arrived several other officials. The scene was at once novel and exciting, as H.M.S. "Actæon" came to an anchor just opposite the city of San Sebastian. The soul-stirring tune of the Brazilian anthem was playing on board the flag-ship, and we were surrounded by vessels of all nations; by gaily-painted passage-boats, by native canoes, by smart little sailing craft, and by Brazilian men-of-war's boats, the crews of which jumped up upon the thwarts at every stroke of the oar.

INHABITANTS OF THE CAPITAL.

The capital of Brazil has been so often described, that, having already sketched the surrounding scenery, I do not care to dwell upon its details. I may, however, briefly mention a few of its more prominent features. Viewed as a whole, it seems to consist of a huge mass of shabby buildings thrown together without any taste or design. Although situated on marshy ground, and usually enveloped in an atmosphere of fever-breeding miasmata, it yet possesses the advantage of overlooking the splendid bay, and of having in its front, on the opposite side, the " Sierra dos Orgaos," those Organ Mountains so often and so justly lauded, and whose sides, as I gazed on them, were clothed with the glories of a golden sunset.

The people who inhabit this unsavoury capital are an indolent race, and are principally made up of " half-breeds." The pure Negro seems to be the most cheerful and industrious of the lot. The inhabitants vary in colour from black to white, or more strictly speaking to whitey-brown. You will see in the narrow dirty streets, darkened by the overhanging upper stories, Mestics, who are the offspring of a white father and an Indian mother; Mulattoes, half white and half Negro, not so prepossessing in their appearance as the former; Creoles, born of Negroes and Brazilians; pure jet black, woolly-haired Negroes from Africa; Caribocoes, half Negro and half Indian; Indians, or aborigines of Brazil, a poor, ugly, and degenerate race; and lastly, not the least important part of the population, the pure Brazilians, who are Portuguese born in Brazil.

Perambulation is by no means easy or agreeable in the muddy streets, which have no pavements or side-paths. They are mostly occupied by Negroes, who are busy everywhere, many of them doing the work of horses. Carrying heavy burdens on their backs they trot along, keeping time to a kind of grunting chorus peculiarly their own. A few lumbering old carriages may be sometimes seen making their way, with difficulty, along streets which are by no means favourable to locomotion. The novel and curious spectacle is diversified by a considerable number of soldiers lounging idly about. There is no lack either of noisy children or of mangy curs; Indians in straw hats are occasionally met; and from time to time stalking solemnly along are priests in sable garments. Not the least characteristic and interesting personages in the crowd are the gay chattering Negresses, with gaudy handkerchiefs bound round their heads, who bear large baskets of bananas, oranges, and guavas.

It is really quite refreshing to leave the Rue da Rieta and stroll into the public garden, on the right of the city, by the water-side, where the rather pretty walks are shaded by umbrageous theobroma and mango trees, and where you feel the comfort of a cool and quiet retreat after the heat, noise, and bustle of the crowded streets.

CHAPTER II.

Land-Crabs and Tiger-Beetles—Inhabitants of an Aloe—Ferns and Flowers—Insects attracted by a Lighthouse—A Useful Aloe—Rockwork—Natural Aquariums—Crabs at Dinner—The Hidden Waters—A Negro Market—The Gold Bug.

To one who delights in the study of the phenomena of nature, in observing the various forms of animal life, in learning the habits and peculiarities of the infinite variety of living creatures, this country is peculiarly interesting. When I for the first time left the crowded town, and wandered along the beach, or penetrated and surveyed the surrounding country, the spectacle on which I looked was at once interesting and exciting. My eye, hitherto so long unaccustomed to see tropical forms of animals and plants, except in the unsatisfactory and oftentimes distorted condition of those in the glass-cases of our Museums, was delighted with the strange sea-eggs, and their no less singular cousins-german, the flattened shield-like clypeasters which, dead and bleached, were strewn along the strand as I jumped ashore at Praya do Tinboy. All around me I beheld numbers of those swift-footed horsemen crabs (Ocypode), which scampered to their holes in the yellow sand when they observed me; and I captured, after exceeding pains and many abortive attempts, about a dozen silvery-white tiger-beetles which, alighting upon the dazzling sand, ran rapidly a little way, and then flew off again.

On all sides rose sombre-tinted granite rocks of colossal magnitude, smooth, and speckled everywhere with lichens white, black, yellow, reddish, and brown. Growing from the fissures of the rocks that skirted the shore, were clumps of huge columnar cactuses, and springing from the sides of yawning gaps, were aloes with dark green, spiky leaves, and flowering stems, twenty, and even thirty feet high. Some of us have read about the strawberry-plant of Saint Pierre, and how he despaired of ever being able to write the history of animals, when he found what time and labour were necessary to study the habits of all the visitants to and dwellers about the leaves and blossoms of the plant on his window-sill. The minute investigation of one of these aloes astonished me almost as much. Little snails, with smooth, yellow shells, called Helicinæ, lurked under the decaying footstalks; creatures, belonging to the bug or hemipterous tribes, of extravagant shapes, reposed on the long green leaves; gigantic spiders called Nephilæ, with very long legs, and gold and silver spotted bodies, hung, head downwards, motionless in the middle of their wide-spread nets, suspended from leaf-point to leaf-point; hairy spiders, short-legged and bloated, guarded jealously their nests, soft, yellow, silken bags filled with spider-babies in the deep-set axils of the leaves; while among the ragged fibres of the root roamed thousand-legs and centipedes!

Leaving the shore and proceeding a little inland, I found myself surrounded on all sides by troops of floral beauties. There were flowers with trumpet-shaped, starlike, and crown-like corollas, whose names were entirely unknown to me. I recognised, however, the sweet, modest, dark-eyed Thunbergia, the bright blue blossoms of Plumbago, and the rich and crimson corymbs of the Asclepias. My "vasculum" was very soon crammed to repletion with the fragile fronds of ferns, the strap-shaped Polypodium squammulosum, the branched Meniscium, the palmate Pteris, and the pretty ash-leaved Anæmia.

One day I paid a visit to the small island of Raza, a conical mass of granite rising from the bottom of the sea; partly bare rock, and partly covered with vegetation. The winds and the waves have, in the course of ages, so acted on the primal mass as to reduce its constituents to powder; and as you walk along you seem to tread on golden dust which is composed of glittering mica. In the deep-blue sky above soared two or three dark, long-winged man-of-war birds, hundreds of restless hungry gulls hovered and screamed around the base, and from his barnacle-clad rock, the red-billed oyster-catcher scanned the stranger with curious eye. As I scrambled up the rough-hewn granite steps, myriads of grey, fork-tailed, sea woodlice swarmed across the path; glistening, brown, golden-eyed lizards darted among the loose stones; little bustling red ants scaled our legs; slender, yellow stone-centipedes lurked in the damp corners; a dark, ugly gecko poked out his warty head to look at us; and a huge, black cockroach gathered around her flattened body a numerous brood, sheltering them carefully as a hen does her chickens. Slow and sober-coloured beetles, called Opatrums, abounded on the barren sandy spots; blue, brown, and yellow butterflies hovered gaily over the convolvulus and Tradescantia flowers that enlivened the sterile ground; and, leaping and whirring among the stunted brushwood, were legions of noisy, long-shanked grasshoppers.

There is a revolving light on the islet, and the bland custodian of the light-house informed me that, attracted by the brilliancy thrown back from his highly polished reflectors, winged insects come by thousands round his lantern, "tapping at his window" all night long.

There is another islet, the precipitous Ilha do Foucinhos, on which our party also landed. There was a little pond at the summit, on the surface of which disported some water-beetles, or gigantic whirlwigs, and crawling on the leaves I noticed a flat, spiral pond-snail, called Planorbis. In lighting a beacon fire, as sailors are fond of doing, our hands grew smutty, and looking round about us, we spied a washing-basin ready made by Nature in the core of an old beheaded aloe, and containing about a quart of clear rain-water! Turkey-buzzards calmly watched our movements from aloft; and, solitary, on a pointed crag, sat a noble, bare-legged falcon, digesting at his leisure some victim of his prowess.

Another day was devoted to the small island named Praya do Vermelha. The heaped-up boulders were crowded with aloes, always hereabout a conspicuous feature in the scene; and the rents and fissures were green with prickly pears. Overcome by the heat, I seated myself on the rocks by the sea, and watched the habits of the creatures peopling the marine aquaria beside me. The stone-basins were filled with translucent water, and fringed with plumose sea-weeds. Purple, long-spined sea-urchins were laboriously crawling up the steep and rugged sides by the aid of their tubular feet; the barnacles, which clothed the submerged surface of the rocks, threw out spasmodically at regular intervals their tufted feet; while above high-water mark, a Littorina (a zebra-striped and beautiful periwinkle) adhered by thousands to the smooth, worn granite. But the crabs amused me most. They nearly all belonged to the genus Sesarma, or painted-crabs, and were very numerous. From the stilly pond they stealthily climbed the rocks just above the wash and ripple of the tide, and once on terra firma, they deliberately scrutinized the weed-clad surface around them. The barnacles were their prey, and they speedily selected one, for their appetite was keen. One set himself down resolutely before the tempting dish. The lids, formed of the opercular valves, were soon removed, and Sesarma luxuriously helped

himself first with one hand and then with the other,
like a greedy boy from a bowl of savoury porridge.
One poor fellow had lost an arm in some fierce fray,
but he plied the remaining member with increased
activity, as if to make up for lost time!

But I have said nothing concerning the mainland,
which, of course, did not remain unvisited or
unexplored. It was a cloudy day when we shot
across the "Hidden Waters," as the Indians call
the harbour, and we rejoiced that the sun so
beneficently veiled his fierce rays in a somewhat
misty atmosphere, for we were bound for the Sugar-
Loaf Mountain, and our toilsome climb would be
more pleasant. As we landed, we found ourselves
among groups of Negroes, squatting on the ground,
and holding a market, with their wares disposed
around them. The shining ebony creatures were
laughing and chattering as is their wont, gaily
discussing each other's merits, and recommending
the flavour of their durians, mammy-apples, and
bananas.

Across the harbour in the far distance to the left,

rose the Organ Mountains, abruptly grand, their many-coloured sides and fluted rocks dimly veiled in the mist of the early morning; while to the left stretched deep purple valleys, and long green undulating hills clothed with an indistinct and billowy verdure.

We had not gone far before the enthusiasm of the party broke forth in exclamations of surprise and delight at the beauty of the scenery, which I confess is quite as attractive as Von Martius and Humboldt have painted it. As we proceeded on our way, we passed a large, weedy, shallow well by the roadside. I looked down into it, and with a covetous eye perceived a flat-backed, long-necked water tortoise, which was leisurely swimming round and round. Suspended above him by a rope was a bucket, which we lowered cautiously, but he persistently refused to enter it. Half afraid of snakes, I penetrated a dense thicket, and crawled on hands and knees to the stems of some wild plantains, meeting by the way all sorts of " clammy, slabby, creeping and uncomfortable life." Under the decaying leaves I found coiled up millipedes of almost fabulous dimensions, and those other flattened forms with sculptured bodies, named Polydesmi. I saw numbers of blue centipedes wriggling away with rapid-moving legs, and snake-like undulations of their many-jointed bodies. Here, too, I found that strange connecting link between the spiders and the scorpions, called by naturalists, Phrynum, a harmless, inert creature, spinning no web, and resembling in its habits the "harvest-men" of English stubble fields. I also came across some living specimens of the curious distorted snail named Streptaxis, which, unlike most land-snails, feeds on worms.

As I emerged again into the brilliant sunlight, I was greeted by the sight of creatures more agreeable and beautiful—the great showy butterflies, languidly flapping their parti-coloured wings.

The botanist, too, will find here specimens of infinite variety for his observation and study. The green-topped tapering palms were splendid, and there were numerous delicate pink-flowered orchids clustering among the branches of the trees. The buff corolla of Thunbergia rivals in its modest beauty the gaudy passion-flowers that hang in rich clusters; and in the dark sequestered nooks many a palmate frond and feathery spray shoot up in all their elegance and beauty.

During our ramble an amusing incident occurred. Some of our party had been reading Edgar Poe's mysterious and imaginative story of the "Gold Bug," and, what is more, actually believed in the existence of such a wondrous insect. As if to confirm them in this belief, and to prove the precious bug to be no myth or fabulous creature of the poet's brain, I captured in my sweeping-net one of those splendid glittering tortoise-beetles named Cassidas, the wings and body of which are fashioned as it were of burnished gold. With laudable pride, I think, and with some exultation, I displayed my prize, but, with questionable veracity, I also proclaimed it to be the veritable "Gold Bug" of the American author. One of my companions, now wandering in the wilds of Borneo, a creature of as heated an imagination as was ever the writer of "the Tales," eagerly scanned the auriferous insect. Desirous of a closer inspection, he insists on holding it in his hand; but no sooner is the envied object deposited in his palm, and his excited gaze captivated by the glitter of its golden wings, than lo! away flies the "gold bug." The utter dismay and blank amazement depicted in the faces of the surrounding group were truly ludicrous. Vain were their regrets at the loss of the precious insect—not another specimen was seen that day; and as we had to start almost immediately on our return voyage, we had no opportunity of capturing another specimen of the same curious species.

CHAPTER III.

The Cape of Good Hope—A Four Days' Beetle Hunt—Millar's Point—Whales' Bones — Fish "galore" — Wrecked Violet-Snails — A Stranded Fiddle-fish—Cormorants and Penguins—Burrowing-Snails—A Vegetable Parachute.

HAVING accomplished the purpose for which we were sent to Rio Janeiro, we left it, on our return, towing the "Dove," our little steam-tender, by two 9-inch hemp hawsers, and after a voyage of six weeks, we reached the Cape of Good Hope. On our arrival the hawsers, which were quite new on starting, were hauled inboard, when they were found covered with barnacles along their whole length. These were nearly all full-grown, and, with the exception of one small white kind of Balanus, were all pedunculated or stalked, belonging to the genera Lepas, Scalpellum and Otion. So numerous were they, that even when the hawsers were comparatively freed from them, they became so offensive, from the decaying animal matter about them, as to require washing with Sir W. Burnett's solution, and they had to be kept on deck a considerable time before they could be reeled up below.

On another occasion we fell in with a floating spar seven hundred miles from the Azores. From the fact of its being covered with barnacles, it was the general impression that it must have been a long time in the water. On a boat being lowered, however, the carpenter examined it, and pronounced it to be a new spar, the lower-mast of some vessel. It was entirely covered with full-grown Lepas anatifera; a fact which goes to prove how rapid is the growth of the Lepades, and also how desirable it is, for the sake of humanity, to examine these floating wrecks, even when they seem apparently hoary with age. The fate of many missing vessels might possibly be determined by reading the name marked upon such floating spars.

The Cape of Good Hope offers in many respects a striking contrast to Rio, yet it is a pleasant place, and I have many pleasant memories of the time passed there. What rambles and scrambles, O Simonsberg, have I not had upon thy rugged sides! What sunny hours have I not spent, among the gleaming, glittering silver-trees! What exciting labour have I not undergone, in overturning huge flat stones for pretty, spotted Anthiæ, and other sand-loving beetles! What thrilling starts have I not experienced at an unexpected sight of a deadly cobra, with head erect and flat dilated neck vibrating rapidly from side to side! With what alarmed surprise have I not found unawares a coiled-up scorpion under a wayside stone! How frantically have I not chased and dodged rock-rabbits among the harsh dry brushwood! How eager have been my quests after the ripe fruits of the fig-marigold! In what triumph have I not borne from the rocky heights above the great showy flowers of Protea magnifica!

The uniform sober features of the Cape are indeed tame after the glowing scenery and exuberant vegetation of Rio; yet the breezy plains covered with heaths and bulbous plants, and the long stretches of brown sandy bays, render a temporary sojourn here very delightful. We remained at the Cape during the whole of the month of April, and found the weather, on the whole, fine, though occasionally somewhat stormy.

One of the author's most lamentable failings is a weakness for beetles; and, as some of my lady readers may wish to know what attraction there is in the pursuit of creatures to them so very uninviting, I will beg them to accompany me in a three-days' beetle hunt.

On landing at Simon's Town almost the first beetle you see in passing through the Dockyard, is a little brown, flat-backed stranger brought over in the sugar-bags from the Mauritius (Tragosita mauritiana). Passing through the town we just loitered to purchase some huge bunches of luscious grapes from Rachel, the pretty fruiterer, and sallied forth rejoicing, to plunge at once among the Proteas which clothed the sides of glorious old Simonsberg. Here, following the example of the long-tailed, gaudy-hued honeysuckers (also partial to beetles), we discovered a rich store of our dingy favourites. In nearly every half-blown blossom we found, smothered in down, a large green sun-beetle, and on proceeding to dissect the overblown flowers, we discovered at least six other kinds, feeding on the floral envelopes or burrowing in the receptacle. On the leaves of the silver-trees, and on the foliage of the heaths, we obtained some pretty lady-birds. Nor were beetles our only companions. On this first day of our hunting season we made the acquaintance of many charming birds, especially of the crow with the white collar, and of the noisy butcher-bird. We picked up a small tortoise, which seemed, poor stupid thing! to have lost its mother; and once we observed with a shudder the sluggish dark form of the fatal cobra glide slowly beneath the shelter of an old uprooted tree.

Another day, ground-beetles were our game. Our fair readers must picture us, covered with sand, toiling among the loose stones at the base of the mountain, turning them over to see what there was beneath. We took some very fine prizes named

Anthiæ, some of which were large and black, some small and white-spotted. Here also we discovered a goodly store of sand-beetles and burrowing shore-beetles. In the gulleys, in the kloffs and small ravines, in the humid neighbourhood of streams and water-courses, mud-burrowing and marsh-beetles, together with a lily-beetle and a few snout-beetles, turned up and rewarded our patient assiduity. The Kaffir herdsman regarded us on this sultry day with special wonder, for while, crouched motionless under the shadiest bush he could find, he watched his browsing buffaloes, lo! we were toiling and moiling in the sun, and after all our exertions finding nothing which we appeared to regard as food! Hence his amazement. On our way back we captured a few stragglers, among them some elongated bark-beetles under the bark of a hollow tree near a pretty cottage on the hillside, where we gathered delicious mushrooms. A fine diving-beetle was taken in a cattle-pond; a mimic flower-beetle and a shard-beetle were captured promenading a sheep-walk. By the sides of a sandy road much used by buffaloes, we came upon a large sable sacred-beetle busily employed, like Sisyphus, in rolling up-hill earthen balls containing his little ones, which, as often as not, when pushed along with his crooked legs nearly to the top of the bank, came rolling down again.

On the third day we proceeded to Millar's Point along the coast, and the special object of our mission was (start not, gentle reader!)—carrion-beetles! We pursued an uneven course up sand-hills and down sand-dales until we espied a huge boulder rock covered with the trailing stems and fleshy leaves of the yellow Mesembryanthemum or Fig-Marigold. The green carpet was torn off from the surface of the stone, when out ran the rove-beetles, large-eyed, burrowing, and broad-bodied. At the same time the little pale scorpions dropped down, while the nimble yellow centipedes vanished mysteriously, with that unpleasant wriggling movement peculiar to hundred-legs and snakes.

About two miles to the left of Simon's Town we crossed a plain where the grass struggled for existence with the sand, and where the round, green gourds of the colocynth rested upon the ground like shot strewing the surface of a battle-field. A thousand footprints of horses stamped in the moist sand (for the ground is used for breaking-in horses,) heightened the resemblance.

On a sudden a taint in the pure air offended our nostrils, but we knew what it meant, and, like the vulture to his carrion-meal, we were led by the nose to the carcase of a sheep! Placing our nobility to windward we capsized the defunct mutton, and those useful scavengers of nature, the burying-beetles and the carrion-beetles, rewarded our bold adventure.

We arrived soon at Millar's Point, and approached the great flat smooth rocks, where, on this wild promontory, they haul up the carcases of captured or stranded whales by chains and windlasses, strip the huge bones of their flesh, and cut up the blubber for the oil. All around were stray fragments and "disjecta membra" of the mighty fish-like mammals. Turning over a dorsal vertebra with effort, for the bone was large and heavy, we secured a choice beetle or two, and by a delicate investigation of an unsavoury fathom of "baleen" we appropriated a shining little skin-beetle.

On our return we descended the sand-hills near the sea, and by the "ancient and fishlike smell" we became aware of the vicinity of a station for cleaning and drying fish. Here were fish galore. Fish salted in great tubs; fish lying in heaps upon the ground; fish by cartloads; fish by boatloads; fish split open on long tables; fish covering all the rocks outside; fish by thousands drying on poles;— stacks of fish! We raised a casual board, and behold, the ground was alive with bombardier-beetles, and there was an irregular salvo as in alarm they discharged their mimic guns!

The long stretch of flat sandy shore between Simon's Town and Fish-hook Bay was a favourite walk of mine, fresh, breezy, and full of interest. The weather had been very stormy of late, and as I strolled leisurely along "the beached margent of the sea" I stumbled across a stranded fiddle-fish,

with a head like a ray and a tail like a shark. The
shore was strewn with many other remnants of fish,
crab, and cuttle, to which various fatal casualties
had occurred. Among these we observed an entire
flotilla of Ianthinas, or violet sea-snails, which had
suffered shipwreck despite the buoyant floats with
which each tiny vessel has been provided by Nature.
Now, however, the scene was very peaceful. Out
at sea only two little boats were visible, fishing for
snook, (a kind of long-nosed mackerel,) between
Noah's Ark and the Roman Rocks. The long rolling breakers came tumbling in with a deep and
hollow roar, and on the huge bare rocks along one
portion of the shore sat the cormorants drying their
dusky wings, or sitting upright, motionless, like
learned doctors met in solemn conclave. Near
them were foolish penguins, gorged with fish,
dozing in the fitful sun-gleams. Three skulls of the
"right whale" were bleaching on the sand, and
the eye of the great sea-eagle watched us from
above.

Strolling a little inland to seek shelter from a

shower among the stunted trees and scrub, I observed hundreds of large globular land-snails suddenly make their appearance on the sandy soil where before the rain they had lain perdu to avoid the heat and dryness of the sun. Here then we had before us a true burrowing snail!

During our brief sojourn at the Cape I was greatly interested in the way in which Nature provides for the dissemination of the seeds of the splendid silver-tree, the Leucodendron argenteum of botanists. The lance-like leaves, the stem, the branches, and even the fruit-cones, are covered with a silky down which glistens in the sun with a silvery sheen, and the mode by which the fruit is dispersed is, as I have said, very curious. The large, oval, silvery cone is covered with scales, which being recurved by the heat, the ripe fruit or seed is suddenly cast forth with a little click. It does not fall at once however to the ground, but is borne up by a beautiful contrivance. The fruit is enclosed in a thin, amber-coloured capsule or case, surmounted by a crown composed of four feathery shafts, which radiate upwards, but are united at their bases to form a sheath for the pistil. When the ripe fruit is ejected from the cone, it bursts the membranous envelope which holds it, and when released falls about an inch, and remains suspended by the stigma, which forms a sort of knot; thus at the same time balancing the tiny parachute, and by its mode of suspension forming a beautiful provision to take off the weight of the parachute when the seed strikes the ground.

CHAPTER IV.

The Gate of the East—Under the Fig Tree—Javanese Market—Monkeys for Sale—Jungle Scene—"Massacre of the Innocents"—Centipedes and Scorpions—The Tiger's Paw—A Ludicrous Incident—Mew Island—Description of a Coral Reef—Gutta-percha Trees—A Deserted Village—Hornbills.

WE were detained some time at "the Gate of the East,"—as the Straits of Sunda have been called—with orders to intercept the troop-ships on their way to China, for we had had tidings of the terrible Indian mutiny, and the troops were wanted elsewhere. We beguiled the time by catching tiger-sharks, and landing on the woody islets which dot the calm deep waters of the sleepy Straits; we shot wild pigs on Thwart-the-way Island, and astonished the noisy cockatoos on Krakatua Island. As we invaded their solitudes, they ascended screaming in large flocks, and circled round and round the highest tree-tops.

At Anger, on the mainland of Java, where we landed on one occasion, we strolled under the shade of the cocoa palms which stretch along the level sandy shore, and watched the artful manners of the sand-crab, which has some very amusing tricks. Near the village we loitered about the great banyan tree, under the shade of whose many-drooping branches and wide-spread foliage cluster the indolent Javanese, in their loose sarongs and bamboo hats, offering for sale their multifarious wares. Squatting on the ground sat a hideous baboon, complacently munching a banana, at the same time keenly watching, with little twinkling eyes (the expression of which was very mischievous), every movement of those around him. Pensive and subdued, hugging his knees with his slender hands, I observed a long-armed ape, while several smaller monkeys, grinning, chattering, and showing their teeth at all who approached them, were quarrelling among themselves, or stealing everything they could lay their hands on. Lories, love-birds, large black and brown squirrels, and Java-sparrows were confined in neat little bamboo cages. Tamarinds and water-melons were exposed for sale. Here and there might be seen a dingy flat-backed water-tortoise, and sometimes a python with splendid spotted skin. Everywhere baskets of the larger and more showy conchs and cowries were so arranged as to attract customers. There were also mounds of cocoa-nuts, heaps of pine-apples, enormous yams, huge bunches of ripe bananas, and numerous aromatic shaddocks which had been grown in the neighbourhood of Batavia, and which always have a finer flavour than any produced elsewhere.

I purchased two pretty spotted civet-cats, which, however, were very unamiable—I may say, savage. I also obtained two of those gentle, timid chevrotins, or pigmy deer, not much larger than hares; they are very difficult to keep alive in confinement, requiring to be fed on thin slices of green plantains, or unripe bananas.

We watered the ship at Mew Bay, near the entrance to Sunda Straits. I went ashore with the watering party, and wandered about to have a look at the place. On the steep, wooded shore I noticed a beautiful little cascade which fell down a rock into the sea; here, under the shade of dark-leaved trees, the water-casks were filled without let or hindrance. There was a legend among the sailors, of a rhinoceros having charged a watering party at this very spot some time previously, which exciting incident, if ever it occurred, lent an additional charm to the spot in the eyes of these danger-loving sons of the sea. In sober truth, however, the ground all about was literally ploughed up by the tracks of these huge unwieldy pachyderms.

Instead of landing at the watering place, however, I preferred making a little *détour* through the forest, at no great distance from the shore. Dead, hoary, lichen-spotted, fern-tufted trunks lay prostrate in my path, and great, green, sombre trees overshadowed the snow-white coral strand, which gleamed beneath their wide-spread orchid-laden branches. My progress at first was somewhat slow and difficult, on account of jungle parasites and thorny creepers; but as I proceeded I looked about and hunted for specimens of natural history. Coming to a fallen tree, I overturned it, and discovered a slender green snake, with a turned-up pointed nose, and otherwise graceful in its movements and appearance. The creature, being vigilant, wide-awake, and active, very naturally made its escape as soon as it found itself disturbed in its retreat. A little further onward I came upon a fallen trunk overgrown with ferns. On raising it I perceived beneath it two ugly scorpions, black, of a formidable size, and coiled affectionately round a numerous progeny. These reptiles were rather repulsive in appearance. With cautious care, for I suspected their venom to be potent, I passed a running noose of twine round their knotted tails, and secured the parents of this interesting family by suspending them to a convenient twig. As for the little ones, I could dispose of them only by a second "Massacre of the Innocents," and every tender scorpion of the brood was mercilessly butchered!

Talking of scorpions reminds me that I have at

times induced some people to believe that I possessed the power of taming these antipathetical creatures, and their equally repellent many-footed relatives, the centipedes. Though the capacity of rendering such venomous reptiles harmless may appear amazing to the uninitiated, there was really nothing supernatural in the "Mystery-man's" black-art, which simply consisted in surreptitiously nipping off the tip of the scorpion's sting and the poison hooks of fell Scolopendra's jaws with a pair of scissors. Thus deprived of the power to penetrate the skin, the once noxious insects are baffled in their attempts to do mischief, and may be permitted to roam undisturbed over the hands and face without the slightest fear of danger.

I next came to a huge tree, which, from its appearance, seemed to promise some response to the anxious inquiries of the naturalist. Its decayed trunk was covered with toadstools, and tenanted by legions of white-ants; we also discovered on it some fungus-eating beetles, a very handsome species, of a goodly size, marked prettily on the back with a black-and-red pattern. Stripping off a portion of the loose and partially-detached bark, I was momentarily startled by the appearance of a little, nimble, dusky, splay-footed, flat-bellied gecko, a sort of lizard, which was instantly taken up and made a prisoner, not, however, alas! without the loss of his tail, which fell off in the struggle. A couple of yellow centipedes were more fortunate in their attempt to escape; dropping on the ground, they vanished in a most desperate hurry. Numerous shining, smooth "thousand-legs" were coiled up in the rotten wood, and under the damp, close-laid masses of bark were the flattened forms of several strange bark-beetles.

This wild tiger-haunted corner of Java is permeated by small trickling rivulets which flow beneath the undergrowth. Stooping down to take a drink at one of these (for the thermometer here stands at 90° in the shade), I noticed something which made me start. Robinson Crusoe, when he saw "the print of a man's foot in the sand," could not have been more completely taken aback than I was by the object on which my eye was riveted. Under my very nose, the fresh imprint of a tiger's paw was manifest, so large that my outspread hand just covered it. Aware, however, of the twilight-loving habits of these cat-like monsters, I felt somewhat reassured, and was by no means inclined to be diverted from my scientific investigations. The finding of some pretty fresh-water shells in the stream diverted my attention from this ominous trace of the much-dreaded man-slayer. It must not be supposed, however, that there was no cause for alarm; two villages in the immediate neighbourhood were at that very moment deserted, having been recently desolated by these formidable animals.

Still, knowing that, though by no means impossible, it was not very likely that they would be prowling about, or venture to make an attack in the full blaze of sunshine, I continued my researches. Among the foliage of the trees I discovered some handsome land-snails, and several other kinds of land-shells under the dead leaves, while pretty silver-marked helmet-beetles alighted on the sunlit blades of horizontal leaves. The loud grating noise of the tree-crickets, or cicadæ, vibrated through the otherwise silent leafy wilderness without a moment of cessation.

A ludicrous incident happened here to my friend B——. Anxious to explore the tiger-haunted precincts of one of the deserted villages, he was confronted on his way by a stream. Nothing daunted, however, by the obstacle, he plunged in and swam to the opposite bank. Here he found a smouldering wood-fire, which he gaily replenished, and before which he hung up his dripping "inexpressibles" on a stick to dry. In the somewhat primitive costume in which he now appeared, he proceeded to examine, with the eye of a hunter, the tracks of rhinoceros and other "feræ naturæ," which, he stated, did greatly abound there. Having satisfied even *his* curiosity, our young friend returned to the bank of the stream to reclaim his nether habiliments. Alas! nothing but a burnt shred was visible. What could he do in these circumstances? No choice remained but to make his way back through the difficult jungle, defiant of scratches, insensible to thorns, eventually to present himself on board, an object of astonishment to his wondering messmates.

A few days later, I spent several hours in exploring Mew Island, a little coral islet near the entrance of the Sunda Strait. This island is densely wooded to the water's edge, and is partly encircled by a barrier-reef. As I stepped from the boat upon the reef, I was struck at once with the extreme beauty of a species of amphitrite, a sea-worm living in holes of the great solid madrepores which compose the reef. The gills of these lovely creatures are in the form of spiral ribbons of a brilliant orange-green and blue; these resplendent gaudy plumes are alternately extruded and withdrawn, and seen through the pellucid water, present a very singular and beautiful appearance. On the moist sand within the reef were numbers of pale grey crickets, veritable maritime Orthoptera, which share the strand with horseman-crabs, and perforate the soil in every direction. It was now calm, as well as hot, and the still water under the dark shadow of the overhanging trees abounded with long-spined purple sea-eggs, glancing here and there among which were black and yellow chætodons, fishes of a strikingly handsome appearance, on account of the contrast of colour which they present. Jumping from stone to stone like so many tiny seals, were numbers of periophthalmi, fish as singular in form as the chætodons are vivid in colour. Sea-slugs, or holothuriæ, were lying quiescent in the shallow pools, or "dragging their slow lengths along" the coral *débris*; some crabs, with bright scarlet eyes, were detected hiding beneath the madrepores; and starfish, with slender snake-like rays, were observed wriggling their way among the dead shells and seaweed. Such were some of the curiosities of nature which struck me as worthy of observation during my sojourn on this tropical barrier-reef.

On penetrating the jungle, I could not but admire the great gutta-percha trees firmly anchored in the loose coral, and supported by broad buttresses which extended beyond the base of their trunks. One giant tree had fallen, and his prostrate form was already clothed with a drooping pall of epiphytes, and nearly screened from view by the pinnate fronds of that fine fern Lomaria, and the cylindric branches of enormous club-mosses, or Lycopodiums. A species of solitary-wasp, and legions of indefatigable white-ants, were engaged on the work of demolition, which in the tropics is soon effected; while in the tree-tops overhead, the cicadæ were chanting a monotonous dirge over the decaying form of the vegetable giant. This was the first time I had seen the Cycas in fruit, and I obtained some fine specimens, of the size and shape of large pine-apples. I perceived also a species of Nepenthes, with very pretty pitchers, growing in great luxuriance in one part of the island.

Continuing my walk, I came upon a deserted village, which offered a picture of mingled luxuriance and desolation—the luxuriance natural, the desolation human. The ruined huts were encircled by verdurous broad-leaved bananas, and the blackened stems of burnt palms, while some were overgrown with ferns, or half buried beneath dense masses of parasitic creepers. The capsicum and cotton-plants around were choked by the rank growth of trailing convolvuli, and the village paths were green with weeds, and obstructed by rotten trees swarming with centipedes and scorpions. Absorbed in the contemplation of this strange scene, I was startled by the sound of heavy, flapping wings, and looking up saw two large birds with outstretched necks, winging their way to a tall bare tree adjacent; as they perched side by side upon it, I recognised the great black-and-white hornbill. In the perfect solitude of the jungle, sudden sounds of mystery, like the vibration of the wings of these birds, the light crafty step of the tiger, or the apprehension of the unknown horrors of the jungle, induce one to carry his hand instinctively towards the faithful revolver. The tigers were very persevering in the pursuit of their prey. Several Malays had come over here to avoid those which had devastated their village on the mainland, but these man-slayers, having once tasted human blood, swam over to the island in pursuit of the fugitives, and so molested them that they were forced to quit the neighbourhood altogether.

CHAPTER V.

A Visit to the Pratas Shoal—The Padi Bird—A Desolate Island—The Joss-House — Lilliputian Forest — Gannets — Rock-Basins — Odd Fishes—Musical Fishes—Ancient Quarries—Banks of the Tchukiang.

My next trip was to the Pratas Shoal, or rather reef, in the China Sea. As the "Dove" gunboat was ordered to survey the reef, I went in her as a volunteer. About one hundred miles from Hong-Kong, a padi-bird was observed on the wing, making futile attempts, poor thing, to get on board. This fact is so far interesting as tending to confirm the theory that, after the aquatic web-footed swimmers like the gulls, the gannets, and the albatrosses, the wading birds form the earliest colonists of oceanic atolls and other far-off islets.

When I landed on the island (which appeared to be merely one end of the horseshoe-shaped coral reef, elevated above the level of the sea, and covered with vegetation), like Robinson Crusoe, I lighted a fire, and made a snug tent-house out of the sail of the jolly-boat, choosing for my bivouac a little sheltered glen, with bushes of Scaviola on one side, and a thicket of stunted Tournefortia on the other. Having appointed one boy as cook, I sent the other boys to collect firewood, and, if possible, to catch a turtle. Having arranged the house to my satisfaction, I took a walk round my island. Fringing it near the sea I observed a carpet of yellowish-green creeping grass, the flowers with large white anthers, and bearing a delicate feathery stigma; and this green circular border was gemmed all over with innumerable blossoms of a pink-and-white convolvulus.

At the first glance nothing is visible inland but dense, rounded masses of glaucous-green shrubs, mostly Scaviola, with here and there traces of Tournefortia. As I advanced, however, I saw open spaces with heaps of finely-powdered coral sand, white as the driven snow. The bones of shipwrecked men, mingled with those of the turtle on which they had fed, were scattered all around, bleaching in the sun. The heat was intense, and with hundreds of gannets hovering over my head, I bathed in the view of the shoreless ocean. So bold grew the gannets as to swoop down upon me, and even to threaten my eyes; and I left the limpid waves to pelt them with lumps of coral, for stones there were none. The dark dorsal fin of a shark appearing now and again above the surface of the water looked ominous and ugly; so I dressed, and proceeded with my explorations.

I had not gone far before I captured a white egret, with a crest of two long feathers; and a gannet's nest which I observed, I robbed of two light green, pointed eggs, as large as those of a duck. In the course of my scientific explorations I was stung by a little scorpion. When I had proceeded some way, I came to a small joss-house filled by grateful mariners with offerings to the Chinese goddess of the sea, this mimic temple having been built by the poor fishers who come here. The fishermen who frequent these coasts catch turtle, and reap a plentiful harvest from the fish-teeming waters which surround the reef. My predilection for the study of nature was here gratified by the sight of several strange creatures. I watched with curiosity the movements of the horseman-crabs, lightly skimming over the level sand on the tips of their toes; and there were numbers of huge brown locusts, everywhere leaping about or spinning round your head with a whirr. A large, downy humming-bird hawkmoth, with rapidly-vibrating wings and fan-like tail, hovered incessantly about the white, many-cleft flowers of the Scaviola Lobelia, which abounds here. On the outskirts of the Lilliputian forest were spread verdant carpets, composed of Crassulaceæ, succulent, thick-leaved plants, watered by the salt spray, among the damp roots of which the land-crabs form large, deep burrows. As I wandered on I came to a shallow lagoon, divided by a tongue of land into two portions. Near the end of it screw-pines or Pandanus, and a few other trees, formed quite a pretty miniature picture of a tropical jungle scene. Madrepore-masses of giant proportions, left high and dry by tempests, fringed one margin of the lagoon. On the coral the pirate-crabs carried about their homes, and numbers of them were maundering on the shore, staggering under their borrowed houses. Wading-birds were fishing the waters of the shallow lake; sandpipers were running over the yielding sands; snipe were probing the oozy mudbanks round the margin; and a few herons eager for crabs were standing on one leg in the middle of the water.

The number of gannets on the island was astounding, the ground in some parts being literally strewn with their eggs. Their nests were shallow, and composed of straws and sticks. In them generally reposed either two eggs, or two unfledged, callow young ones, with greedy eyes, big heads, and gaping mouths, straining their necks for food. Their mothers stood around; and I noticed that the contents of the pelican-like pouch they carry under their bills chiefly consisted of flying-fish, the flavour of which the hungry infant-gannets appeared fully to appreciate.

The "Actæon" proceeded to Hong Kong, where

she remained for some time. While we were there, my companions and myself were accustomed to get up very early in the morning, and walk to Pok-fo-lum, about two miles distance, for the sake of bathing in the rock-basins there. In one place, a mountain torrent rushing down the deep ravine had worn away the softer portions of the rocks, and hollowed them out into deep basins full of cold limpid water constantly supplied by numerous mimic waterfalls. In these it was our delight to dive and swim, or to sit under the waterfalls. The perfect quiet of the place offered a strange contrast to the hubbub and bustle which greeted us on our return into the town, where all were wide awake by this time, busily engaged in their several occupations; the swarthy smith hammering on his anvil; the fruiterer cutting up his water-melons; the tailors squatting on their haunches; the barbers shaving their customers' heads, ears, and eyelids; and quack doctors eulogising their wondrous remedies.

This early hour is the time to pay the fish-mongers a visit. Their ample boards are now covered with the proceeds of the thousand fishing craft that daily crowd the offing. The fish exposed for sale are not such as we see in fishmongers' shops at home. In huge tubs swimming crabs and marbled cray-fish are kicking and pushing each other; flying-fish and bonitos, lovely even in death; monster congers, with horrid teeth and pointed jaws; crimson-spotted flat-fish, rough spiny rays, and huge mis-shapen skates; snaky marbled eels; glittering silver perch, with sharp spiny fins; here and there a rough brown shark, with evil eye and grinning mouth; file-fishes and cow-fishes, in their shagreen coats-of-mail, and bodies cased in bony plates; spotted dog-fishes and dragonets; blenny-bullheads, with beards hanging from their lips; silvery, bright, clean-looking scabbard-fishes, with pointed chins; the shining dollar-fish, the red and grey gurnards, with their great spiny, armour-plated heads; and the sluggish, freshwater, whiskered cat-fishes.

My next "fishy" experience occurred while the "Actæon" was lying off Macao, near the entrance of the Pearl River, where every evening the drum-fishes assembled around the vessel, and continued their musical humming till about midnight. My messmate in the next cabin called out, "There go the drum-fishes;" and I would lie awake and listen to their monotonous drone on the other side of the planks which separated me from them. The noise rose and fell, and sometimes suddenly ceased; and the band of performers seemed to disperse, as they sought their food among the barnacles which encrusted the bottom of the vessel. "Mute as a fish" is certainly very expressive, and, as a rule, moreover, is generally true, though I have heard toad-fishes grunt pretty loudly when taken out of the water. "A fish up a tree" seems almost an impossible thing; but have we not all heard of the climbing perch of India? "A fish out of water" appears strange and unnatural; but blennies, with protruding eyes and jointed pectorals, are seen hopping about the muddy banks of Chinese rivers, and perching on stray logs like any frogs. With fishes that fly or suspend themselves we are all familiar; and that certain denizens of the deep are enabled, by means at present unknown, to produce sounds under water, is a fact no less certain, being well known to sea-faring men. Captain Ward tells me that the "drum" is familiar to the inhabitants of Charlestown in South Carolina. When he was lying off that place in the "Thunder," mysterious humming sounds were heard from time to time proceeding from the bottom of the ship. These sounds were generally ascribed to insects in the spirit-room. One day, however, some ladies visited the ship, and on hearing the peculiar vibrating noise, exclaimed, "Ah, there's the drum-fish!" They described it as of large size, and declared the roe was considered a great delicacy.

For many following months we remained anchored in various portions of the Canton River, and took advantage of our stay to explore several places of interest, notwithstanding the known treachery of the natives, and the desultory kind of warfare we were now engaged in. I accompanied on one occasion a land-exploring party to the ancient granite quarries, from the granite of which the walls of the old city of Canton and the numerous huge river-forts were constructed long, long ago. At present the quarries form vast, gloomy caves and over-hanging, even-fronted, water-dripping rocks. The enormous moss-grown boulders and the heaped-up masses of old-world lichen-stained granite encompass you on every side, and you seem to be surrounded by the handiwork of Titans. All is silent, damp, and sombre. In the dark, deep pools the harmless water-snakes swim gracefully over the still surface, or dive beneath the water. The time-worn caverns and shady nooks, overgrown with foliage, are the favoured haunt of the brown owl and the grey soft-plumaged goat-sucker, which startle us as they fly out suddenly from the deep silent chasms of the rock. I was much impressed on this occasion with the harmony of colour which exists between animals and the places in which they reside. A slender lizard, of a brownish-green colour, is hardly to be distinguished from the blades of grass among which it habitually takes up its abode; and a creature somewhat allied to him, and named gecko, is so freckled and spotted and blotched with brown, and umber, and bistre, that you can hardly separate him from the surface of the weather-stained granite rocks in the chinks and crannies of which he passes his existence.

All around these ancient quarries frown down upon us barren, red-tipped hills, rough with scraggy fir-trees, and crested here and there with wind-bent pines. On a brown, fissured, rounded hill a tall, shapely pagoda rises conspicuous, and half buried in a sacred grove at the base is an old many-gabled, dragon-invested joss-house or temple, picturesque, quaint, and eminently Chinese; while, indistinct in the far distance, are the pale grey lofty mountains.

The banks of the Chu-Kiang, or Pearl River, are planted at regular intervals with the dark-leaved li-chee and peach-trees now covered with blossom, agreeably relieved with chili bushes and clumps of the pale green, broad-leaved plantain; while the level padi-fields, half under water, are yellow with heavy-cared rice. The broad river flows calmly by. Here and there, stretched out athwart the stream, are countless fishing-stakes, extending in regular, long rows, with black fishing-nets drying in the sun, and arranged in festoons on the ropes which stretch from pole to pole. Little sampans are floating like so many waterfowl on the water, drifting with the current, and paying out their fishing-lines furnished with a hundred baited hooks; poor villagers, dusky, half-clothed figures, are patiently seeking for cat-fish, or groping for mussels on the river banks which the tide leaves bare; up little narrow creeks cluster hundreds of brown dome-roofed fishing craft, while conspicuous over the low land are the tanned square sails of the trading junks sailing along the distant reaches of the winding river.

I ascended a neighbouring hill, and from the summit surveyed the beauty, fertility, and teeming population of this "Central Flowery Land." The brown sides of the old, old granite hill on which I stood were pitted with innumerable graves of the humbler classes, and honeycombed with the tombs of the wealthy. The modest graves, and the more pretentious moss-grown tombs, were overrun and partially concealed by the small-flowered bramble, the wild rose, and the yellow chrysanthemum, while vines clung here and there in graceful festoons, and clustered about the angular rock-masses and the scattered rounded boulders. Stretched below were green, fertile plains, dotted with villages more numerous than the eye could count, standing boldly out, or sheltered in groves of dark evergreen fig-trees. The rich alluvial plains were green with garden stuff, or golden with the ripe waving fields of padi, and all were watered by canals and intersecting rivulets, like the water-meadows of England on a gigantic scale.

CHAPTER VI.

An Apology for Beetles—Village Trees—The Buffalo and the Fanqui—Danes Island—Boy Hunters—Habits of Ants—Flowers compared with those of England—North and South, a Porcine Contrast—Reservoirs in Canton—Monster Aquarium—Pond Shell-fish—The Scaly Ant-eater—Master Wouff and "Scales."

ON approaching the villages I saw the hanging branches and dark foliage of the shining fig-tree (Ficus nitida), and the hoary limbs of the great Bombax Cepa, entirely bare of foliage, but covered with magnificent scarlet flowers. The bamboos were really grand, the finest I had ever seen. Under the clumps of this huge grass, which here grows forty feet high, I found a pleasant shelter from the sun, and—a few beetles. Among them a pale yellow kind, a giant among lady-birds. On the ground, among the dead leaves, rustled a glistening brown lizard, and about the roots mole-crickets ran timidly along, or lazily scraped the moist earth with mole-like paws. As for beetles, they abounded everywhere!

Perhaps it may seem absurd to lavish praise and bestow regard upon creatures not usually viewed with feelings of love or admiration, but I must again confess I have a liking for beetles. "A beetle is a beauty in the eye of its mother," says the Arabic proverb, and, I may add, in the eyes of the entomologist also. Be that as it may, I shall add here that, in whatever direction I looked, I found wonderfully fashioned creatures of this tribe, shining and bejewelled, and nicely adapted to the place of their abode. Under the surface of the bamboo leaves I observed the giant lady-bird; in the grass lurked a spiny tortoise-beetle; clinging to the stems was a black and red flower-beetle; on the wing disported a bright little unicorn-beetle; on the ground crept a soberly bedight, soft-brown chaffer; on the stones shone a glittering gold-beetle; under the oolam trees I discovered a dull-green fellow; on the trefoil leaves in the sunny pea fields were sun-beetles and gold-beetles. Besides these were a large red Horia and a perfect little gem of a Callistes.

At the period of my visit it was the season of the green leaf and flower. The low wooden houses were environed by the guava and the orange tree, their boughs bent down with grateful fruit. Mingled with these were the dark-leaved fig-tree, the privet-like Ancistrobolus, the rich purple leaves of the Psychotria, and the Gardenia florida, always a favourite with the Chinese on account of its fragrant flowers. These village trees were haunted by yellow-banded wasps, and heavy-bodied sawflies. Lurking among the foliage were golden-spotted beetles, while, poised in mid-air, on vibrating wings, were clear-bodied flies and bee-like insects named Bombylii. Artfully disposed among the bristling thorns of a Palinurus bush, I espied the nest of a little slender brown bird, well defended and snug, bidding defiance to snakes and other harmful creatures.

As I returned to the ship I observed a water buffalo plodding steadily across a padi field, the rude wooden plough turning up the soil behind her. These unlovely, mud-incrusted ruminants seem to think with the Turk that "of all devils the very worst of devils is a Frank in a round hat," for no sooner does the unwieldly creature scent the "Fanqui," than she stops abruptly, snorts, trembles, and—is off! Nose in air, and horns flat back, she splashes through the watery glebe, the plough at her tail. The vexed Chinaman gazes helplessly after his unruly charge, but, soon, to the great relief of the unfortunate husbandman, up comes a little boy who whispers soft nonsense in the vagrant's ear, and leads her back, a willing captive, by the rope made fast to the cartilage of her nose.

Danes Island, like all the other islands in the river, rises from the bed of the Chu-Kiang as a primary granite-mass. Its green rounded hills are covered with a scanty vegetation, and pitted with the scooped-out graves of many generations of Chinese. A layer, more or less deep, of red and white sandstone, rests upon the granite, and between the hills are valleys with a rich alluvial bottom, where pumpkins, melons, rice, peas, beans, ground-nuts, and sweet potatoes form vast vegetable gardens. The terraced sides of the more barren hills are planted with the oolam or olive, the li-chee and the peach. The villagers are harmless, but now and then get into trouble for supposed insults to the British flag, but what then?—"Every day is not a Feast of Lanterns."

Under the shade of the dark-leaved firtrees, where repose the dead of the mild, intelligent Parsees, I loved to sit upon a gravestone and feast on the cool, pink flesh of water melons. While I was thus regaling myself on one occasion, a brown, pig-tailed, bare-legged urchin came panting, almost breathless, up the hill. He bore a home-made bamboo-box, to which a crumpled leaf served for a cork. This he eagerly withdrew as he approached me, and revealed the head of a large yellow centipede, whose unpleasant body seemed very much inclined to follow. This entomological capture, offered with a smile of conscious pride, was a present for the "Esung." These village urchins were great allies of mine. They showed as much ardour in the chase as any naturalist, nor could a legion of Ariels have served their master Prospero better than these dusky imps did me.

When, with their narrow gleaming eyes, they saw me discard the "disjecta membra" of the great black copris, the dung of the buffalo was forthwith scattered to the winds, and dozens of the living beetles were disentombed and brought to me. They knew the haunts of skink, mouse, bird, and beetle. Did I desire an ant-lion? They were immediately under the oolam trees, blowing away the sandy soil with their breath, till they spied the lurking lion in his den, hiding in a hole on one side of the pitfall, his long powerful jaws being just visible in the centre. As they scratched him out they sang a little ditty appropriate to the occasion. Did I want a frog? A slight pencil sketch of the creature was shown them, and off scampered these pig-tailed Ariels, returning in ten minutes with as many frogs as would feast a dozen Frenchmen. Infants of tender years would join in the sport, and when success had crowned their efforts, would toddle up bashfully with a locust or some other prize struggling in their tiny paws. One little fellow was bitten by a large spider which he had courageously seized, and, as he presented his captive, he pointed with tearful eyes to his swollen finger.

The ants of this island are a very interesting study. One species of a yellowish hue, with very long legs and antennæ, builds large nests in the oolam trees by bending down and joining together the leaves. The jaws of these ants are strong and toothed, and pierce the edges of the leaves, when a viscid sap exudes, which soon hardens in the air, and cements the leaves together. Another ant, with a roundish body covered with a grey pubescence, forms cylindric holes in the ground, with an elevated tubular shaft an inch or more above the surface, composed of grains of sand. Another solitary ant jumps about the pathways like a Saltica, or hunting-spider. This is a curious elongated species, with a great head and thorax, and with the mandibles produced in front, forming a long pair of forceps, curving slightly upwards. My friend Mr. Frederick Smith, to whom I presented a specimen, told me its name, but I have forgotten it.

Although not specifically the same, the flowers I met with in my walks reminded me of those in England. The Oxalis is yellow-flowered, and does not produce so pleasant an acid as our own wood-sorrel; the shepherd's-purse appears to be the same as ours; the groundsel is represented by Emilia sonchifolia; the Persicaria is replaced by Polygonum chinense; the woolly Gnaphalium resembles that which grows in waste places in England; instead of the harebell we have here the Wahlenbergia agrestis; and in place of the bindweed, we find the Evolvulus emarginatus, with its trumpet-like flowers. By the margin of a running stream, springing in numbers from the fresh green sod, I saw the Spiranthes australis, a delicate little orchid reminding one of S. æstivalis and familiar Hampshire meadows.

In the deep, damp fissures of the ground, the

red coral-like corymbs of Ixora stricta were conspicuous; and on the white dilated calyx-segments of Mussænda erosa I found clustered a pretty beetle called Hoplia, with a silvery-grey pubescence. The long segments of the crimson-spotted flowers of Strophanthus arrested *my attention as I approached the precincts of a village, and I stopped to gather the sweet-scented corymbs of Clerodendron fragrans. I also sniffed an odour not so pleasing, and peeping over a bamboo fence I observed a piggery! And this fact reminds me of the great difference between the social and physical condition of the pigs of the north and the pigs of the south of China. The pig of the south lies in a clean sty, and is well cared for. She has a short, wrinkled face, glutton eyes, swollen cheeks, a sunken back, short legs, and a pendulous belly, and she waddles stolidly along with a kind of semi-somnolent complacency. The pig of the north, on the contrary, has to take care of himself, and judging from his *physique*, he is able to do so. He is a black, hirsute, active and irascible pachyderm, with a lean body, long legs, a wedge-like head, a bristling crest, an inquisitive nose, a wicked, vigilant eye, a straight tufted tail, and a shrill, angry voice.

The numerous ponds within the walls of the city of Canton are intended as reservoirs of water in case of fire. They are by no means filthy or muddy receptacles, but resemble in beauty and cleanliness the parlour ponds and aquatic vivaria of our gardens on a large scale. The surface is covered with a mass of bright green floating vegetation; while the margins are fringed with crisp and juicy esculent vegetables. The water below teems with carp, dace, and other fish which live upon the fresh-water mollusks, these in their turn feeding on the superabundant vegetable matter. The pond shell-fish consist of a species of Sphærium, and one or two kinds of Vivipara, or Paludina. One of the fish, a species of Ophiocephalus, has no teeth in the jaws, but the pharynx is provided with a pair of powerful supplementary maxillæ armed with formidable serrated teeth, which play against a hard, rough, bony palate, and so crush the shells of the mollusks on which it feeds.

Seen from the porcelain pagoda, these verdurous ponds appear as oases in a desert of tiles.

Two living specimens of the scaly ant-eater (Manis javanica) having come under my notice, some account of its habits, as far as I was enabled to make them out, may be acceptable. The first was a female, and rejoiced in the sobriquet of "Scales." She was crepuscular, and remained coiled up in a ball during the day, secure in her scaly panoply. At the approach of night, however, she grew lively. A creature whose habits require to be studied by the aid of a dark lantern, must needs be interesting even to the most incurious observer; and a lizard-like mammal, whose every movement and attitude is probably a living illustration of those great extinct quadrupeds which once peopled the earth before man was created, must surely have the power of arresting the attention, if not of stimulating the imagination, of all who desire to penetrate the secrets of Nature.

I doubt not Professor Owen would have lain prone on his stomach all the livelong night to watch the evolutions of this gnome-like mountaineer, in whose aspect, as she prowled about at night, there was something old-world and weird-like. The Scotch would say she had an "uncanny" look; and truly, if but ten times bigger, she would have unmistakeably reminded one of the times before the Deluge. When she walked, she trod gingerly on the bent under claws of her fore feet, and more firmly on the palms of her hind feet. A very favourite attitude with her was that assumed by her gigantic extinct analogue, the Mylodon, as seen in the wondrous model of Waterhouse Hawkins in the gardens of the Crystal Palace. The fore-feet in my "Madam Scales" were raised; and the animal was supported by the strong hind limbs, and the firm, flattened, powerful muscular tail, the head and body being at the same time moved from side to side, and the little round prominent eyes peering cautiously about in every direction. In walking, the fourth toe of the hind foot was also extended. The Chinese, in their sly manner, said that she pretended to be very quiet; but "s'pose no man lookee," she run very fast. She was certainly of an exceedingly timid and retiring disposition, tucking in her head between her fore-legs on the least alarm. So apathetic a quadruped appeared our "Pangolin" (for so was she called by the Malays), that, coiled up in a strong net, I considered her properly secured, and carefully deposited her in my cabin. No sooner, however, had the last gleam of light vanished from my little "scuttle," than she knew the period of her lethargy had expired, and, bursting the trammels of her hempen toil, she roamed abroad. The first intimation I had of her escape was the ominous bark of Master "Wouff," a clever little terrier on board. The dog, puzzled by the queer scaly rat he had suddenly encountered, regarded with impotent rage the lizard-like intruder; while "Scales," secure in her coat of mail, bid defiance to the attacks of her canine assailant.

The scaly ant-eater is called by the Chinese of Quang-tung, "Chun-shau-cập," which literally means "Scaly hill-borer." They also name it "Ling-li," or "Hill-carp." It seems to be regarded by them as truly "a fish out of water," though it lives in the sides of the great mountains. They say it lays a trap for insects by erecting its scales, which suddenly closing on the entrance of flies, ants, &c., these intruders are secured, and, when dead, fall out and are eaten. It is also said to feed upon fish; but both these stories appear to be myths, something similar to those told of our own familiar "hedge-pig" sucking the teats of cows, and impaling apples on her quills in the orchards.

The Manis javanica is sold in the markets at Canton, and is often carried about the streets as a curiosity. The scales are employed by the Chinese for medicinal purposes; but the flesh does not appear to be eaten, though it is very excellent food when roasted, as I can testify from personal experience, having had a portion of the defunct "Scales" cooked. The Manis climbs very well, and can suspend itself head downwards by means of its strong flat tail. We fed our "Scaly hill-borers" on raw eggs and chopped raw beef, on which they seemed to thrive. The unfortunate "Scales" fell a victim to female curiosity. Exploring the hold of the ship in one of her midnight rambles, she was lost for a time, and though she at length found her way back to her box, she was so exhausted by long abstinence that she died of starvation.

CHAPTER VII.

Stroll through Villages on the Yang-tsze-Kiang—Spring-time—The Pupa Gatherer—How to fatten Ducks—Characteristic Scene—Banks of the Great River—Freshwater Crabs—Eriocheir Japonicus—Youthful Poachers—The Mina Bird—Adventures of a Thousand-legs.

A STROLL through the straggling villages on the banks of the Yang-tsze-Kiang is pleasant enough in the spring. Along the level bund, coolies are carrying burdens at the end of bamboos, rich men are riding in couples on wheelbarrows, a little-footed woman is toddling awkwardly along, and a shaven priest in a dingy robe is stalking solemnly by. The peculiarity of their appearance, and the novelty of their costume, at once interest and amuse the stranger.

Inland is seen a vast, green, cultivated plain, with scattered farms and hamlets, and their attendant white goats and hungry yelping curs. An aged

crone is usually spinning at the open door. There
are ducks in the dykes which always encircle the
houses, and in the elm and willow trees are the
familiar magpies and mina-birds. As the fields are
now dry, rice, padi-birds, and frogs are gone; not
even a land-crab sidles along the muddy banks.
All around the yellow blossoms and snowy pods of
the cotton are mingled with the foxglove flowers of
Sesamum, from the seeds of which an oil is expressed. Wheat and barley form undulating fields,
together with purple tares and sweet-scented flowering beans. A granite arch, dedicated to filial
piety, often rears its quaint form above the cotton-
fields, and everywhere wooden coffins are seen exposed in the open air. The grassy grave mounds
are yellow with Chrysanthemum chinense, and from
them is heard the sibilant song of the grasshopper-
lark. The pheasant crows in the young corn, and
the pretty ringdove flies across the path to join her
mate in the bamboo thicket.

The banks of the river are covered with violets
and dandelions, mixed with patches of yellow

Thaumatopsis, and, what is rare in these southern latitudes, with the blue flowers of a little gentian. The aspect of the country, on the whole, suggests a favourable view of the people; the scene presented is one of smiling plenty. The natives, evidently an industrious race, are everywhere busy, and may be seen tending their goats, weeding their crops, or threshing out the last year's padi. While the women are carefully tending the cotton plants, the men are engaged in the more laborious occupation of turning the sod, and crushing the clods with their heavy four-pronged hoes, the children at the same time gathering esculent leaves.

Turning my eye in one direction, I perceived an individual with basket on arm, surveying the willows with inquiring eye. I was curious to know on what he was intent, and observed his motions. By means of a little sickle at the end of a long bamboo he ever and anon detached brown swinging cradles from the slender boughs, and deposited them in his basket. I learned from himself that he was a pupa-gatherer, and that those tiny mummy-like objects of his solicitude were the pupa-cases of a species of moth. When I humbly desired to know the use to which these accumulated grubs were to be put, the face of the old man relaxed into a smile, and he did his best to assume the appearance of a duck gobbling up imaginary fat grubs with impatient greediness and noise. From this pantomime I gathered that he was collecting food for his ducks; for this is one of the several ways which they have of fattening ducks in China.

In the beginning of summer, when the Principia utilis, which in winter time is nothing but a tangled mass of green thorns, teems with milk-white flowers, and swarms with bees; when the edges of the narrow paths are gay with the white and pink coronals of Anthyllis, about which wasps are flying, vigilant and bustling; when in all waste places the blue flowers of Veronica mingle with the milk-white stars of Stellaria, and in the far distance a puce-coloured mass of peach blossoms contrasts with the green willows; when those long-beaked hairy flies, the bombylii, hover over the hot narrow paths, like so many lilliputian humming-birds, and yellow-legged bees settle on the sun-bright spots; then you are startled in your walks by strange guttural noises which seem to come from beneath your feet, but which proceed in reality from the iris leaves that margin the river's brink. There, moored in some secluded shallow spot, is seen a long-roofed boat, shaped like Noah's Ark, with a sloping board leading into the reeds and sedges. A little boy watches all day long his greedy charges, keeping them in order by means of a slender wand with a bit of rag at the end. At daybreak down swarm the ducks into the frog-peopled swamp, and at sunset they are driven back, and waddle up the ladder by which they gain access to their roosting place.

There is a wide marshy plain at the junction of the Woosung and Yang-tsze rivers, with mudflats stretching away for miles. Here the uncouth buffaloes delight to wallow in the ooze; the white padi-birds stand in a row at the edge of the water; and far in the distance, like a sentry at his outpost, watches the gray solitary heron. A flock of teal settles down in the water, and the sparkling surface of the river is dotted with brown-sailed junks. A vole or field-mouse sometimes runs across your path, or the gliding form of a snake is seen vanishing in the grass.

Towards evening, frogs are demonstrative, croaking loudly and without cessation, and leaping by hundreds down the banks of the dykes and streams. Now these merry batrachians are good for ducks, and Chinamen are particularly fond of *fat* ducks. The natural result is that, at this "witching hour of night," silent boys and old patient men are seen in these frog-haunted precincts, a long bamboo rod in their hand, and a string baited with a worm, angling for frogs! In my homeward walks, when the brown owl swooped down and settled on the cotton fields, and the huge black shard-beetle flew across my face, I often fell in with an old man bending under the weight of a hamper of frogs, the produce of his evening's fishing.

On the banks of the Great River are tracts of low swampy land, irreclaimable even by the patient industry of the Chinese husbandman. These tracts are haunted by curlews, snipe, and plover, while water-buffaloes, attended by groups of noisy mina-birds, alternately ruminate and wallow in the mire. Scattered over these swampy plains are certain sedgy pools, the water of which, though it looks black, is very clear. The bottom is of soft mud, and from it grow the reed, the iris, and the bullrush, fringing the peaty margin. Over their emerald swords and spears often hangs the little blue-backed kingfisher, and up to his knees in water stands watchfully the snow-white padi-bird. In these ponds there is no lack of fish, and their waters are peopled with noisy frogs. Some portions of the adjoining ground are pierced like a colander with holes, which are the work of the "crab with a bloody hand!"

As in England boys take possession of ponds, moorlands, and commons, and disport themselves therein, not only robbing the humble-bee and stoning the frogs, but causing much trouble and uneasiness to the gamekeeper—so do the urchins of the Flowery Land resort to these oozy pools for useful sport or idle recreation. With an artfully-fashioned wicker basket, narrow at the top and sloping at the sides, the pig-tailed boy advances cautiously into the yielding mud, probes with his toes the overhanging banks, or plunges both his arms beneath the spongy roots. The object of his search, when captured, is adroitly transferred to the basket hung about his neck, and on examination turns out to be the Eriocheir japonicus, or the "crab with a hairy hand." This creature is of a dark olive hue, freckled and flat-backed, apathetic in his disposition, by no means nimble on his pins, nor aggressive with his hirsute claws. Placed on the ground, he shambles along sideways towards the water, never moving in an inland direction, and, when possible, speedily makes himself invisible beneath the soft black mud. Strolling through the unsavoury purlieus of the village of Woosung, I noticed in all the fish-shops long strings of these crabs, which, from their abundance in the market, seemed to be admired articles of diet among the poorer Chinese. For half-a-mace I purchased two strings, each of nine full-grown "crabs with the hairy hand."

※ ※ ※ ※

In many a sunshiny walk to the Bubbling Wells or to the Pagoda, my only and nearly constant companions were the mina-birds and the poor worm whose peculiarities I have described below. I was familiar with these two all the way there and back again, for the huge-bodied buffalo and the yelping dog, the oblique-eyed child or the little-footed woman, were but casual roadside acquaintances.

The sky at this time of the year (the month of March), and when the weather is fine, is of a pale blue, and the fields, with their fresh crops of young wheat, are of a beautiful emerald-green. At this period the first swallow makes its appearance, harbinger of spring, always welcomed with joy. The quaint little children spread over the fields, which are not enclosed by hedges, were always to me a most pleasant and amusing spectacle. They were constantly busy, filling their small baskets with every esculent leaf and blade not sown by man. The Compositæ and Cruciferæ were the principal objects of their search, the knowing urchins carefully avoiding deleterious Euphorbiaceæ.

In this part of China the myriapod crawls in every sunny path; and in the air above hum the early andrænas—for the other bees are not yet out—diligently seeking, with steady zigzag flight, their food in every flower. At this early period, the insect world is not yet fairly roused from its winter sleep. A glittering black Staphylinus occasionally alights upon the path, a dull Aphodius falls down before you, or an adventurous land-crab makes an experimental trip from one hole to another on a sunny mud-bank. The dykes are filled with little pellucid fish, with big heads and large golden eyes.

As for the mina-bird, he is everywhere. As you pass through the settlement, a loud cheery note salutes your ear, and on looking about to thank the feathered vocalist, you see, perched upon the cornice of the tallest house, a mina, solitary, but apparently on good terms with himself, piping at intervals in the fulness of his joy. While the old women are sitting in groups before their doors, busy with their spinning and their cotton-pods, the mina-birds dispute the crumbs with the ducks and the fowls. Among the buffaloes in the marsh by the river's brink, familiar and noisy, they gather in little flocks, perching on the heads and backs of their flat-horned, mud-covered companions, or refresh themselves by making short excursions to the adjacent homesteads. From the bamboo and fir-tree plantations, which make the temples so picturesque, issue forth their clear, sweet notes, mingled with the impudent "quirk, quirk" of the magpie, the harsh screech of the long-tailed butcher-bird, the noisy chatter of the blue jay, and the familiar chirp of the homely sparrow.

On every path, where the sun is at his brightest, the myriapods, or thousand-legs, may be seen urging their way onward, "with a heart for any fate." Like their brother worms with legs less numerous, they are supremely ignorant of the sayings and doings of the powers above, and preferring the dry sunny paths to the scented bean fields and the shelter of the cotton-plants, they get crushed under the Juggernaut wheels of Chinese hand-barrows, or beneath the ponderous tread of labouring coolies. Differing in this respect from most of his consimilars, who are of retiring habits, and love the seclusion of rotting logs, or seek the shelter of stones, our myriapod seems to love the sun. It is always curious to watch his movements. The great hulking spider which he encounters jerks himself out of the way; he goes without flinching through the serried ranks of a little foraging party of ants, or, if he cannot go through them, he marches over them; fissures, which to him must be frightful chasms, he boldly encounters; hillocks, in his eyes rugged mountains, he faces and surmounts with ease. With unfailing energy he works his "myriad" legs, seeking in his progress—who knows what? To me, who have so often watched his wanderings, his object still seems purposeless: I have not fathomed the mystery of his life. Unheeded, he passes by the charming bells of Mazus pulchellus, a pigmy beauty, whose blossoms nearly touch the earth; he pushes under bits of straw and withered blades of grass; he evades the fallen cotton pods, the beards of barley, and the awns of rice; he disregards the thistle-down and the feathered seeds that lie in his way; he will reject a putrid land-crab, and turn up his (metaphorical) nose at a dead snail; he inclines towards a crushed fungus, but on second thoughts is not partial to toadstools; he makes for a decayed fragment of wood, but he does not banquet on that. As he crawls, he perpetually forms "lines of grace and beauty," by the lateral undulations of his mobile body. I have named him Craspedosoma vagabunda!

CHAPTER VIII.

Miatau Islands—Probable Origin of some Stories about Sea-serpents—Alceste Island—Seals—Fishing Cormorant—The Blue Rock-pigeon—Kala-hai—A Fishing Party—Bustards—Snake-like Fishes—Gulf of Pecheli—Strange-looking Craft—Native Fishermen—A Shower of Beetles—The Black Surf-Duck.

WHILE on board the ship of which I was surgeon, an incident occurred which, I think, deserves to be recorded as an illustration of optical delusion that might have become a source of error, and given rise to yet another story of the famed sea-serpent. We were sailing among the islands of the Miatau group, at the entrance of the Gulf of Pecheli. There was little wind, and gentle ripples covered the surface of the sea. I was sipping my Congou at the open port of the ward-room on the main deck, and while I was admiring the setting sun, watching the rounded outlines of the blue mountains and distant islands against the sky, and wondering at the number of sea-birds wheeling rockwards to their nests, my eye rested on a long dark object apparently making its way steadily through the water. After observing it some time in silence, I was sorely puzzled, and could make nothing of it. As it was evidently neither a seal, a diver, nor a fishing cormorant, with the forms of which I was familiar, I went on deck to consult other eyes than my own. Sundry glasses were brought to bear on the suspicious-looking object, and after long scrutiny it seemed to be generally decided that it was a large snake, about ten feet long (much longer, according to some,) working its way vigorously against the tide by lateral undulations of the body. So strong was this conviction, that the course of the ship was altered, and a boat was got ready for lowering. With a couple of loaded revolvers, some boat-hooks and a fathom or so of lead-line, I made ready for the encounter, intending to range up alongside, shoot the reptile through the head, make him fast by a clove-hitch, and tow him on board in triumph! By this time, however, a closer and more critical inspection had taken place, and the supposed sea-monster turned out to be, in reality, a long dark root of a tree, gnarled and twisted, and secured to the moorings of a fishing net; the strong tide passing it rapidly, giving it an apparent life-like movement and serpentine aspect.

* * * * *

"Alceste Island,"—the name of which recalls the splendours of a former Embassy to China, and many pleasant associations connected with the Narrative of Staunton, and the Voyages of Captains Maxwell and Basil Hall, not forgetting Surgeon Macleod's "Voyage of the Alceste,"—is a little high island, placed to the north of the extremity of the Shan-tung Promontory, the easternmost continuation of the lofty peninsula which forms the Province of Shan-tung. On the rocks above water which form a portion of the reef that extends about a mile round the island, lie huddled together numbers of seals, which, on our approach in the boat, all tumble off into the water. The fishing cormorant evidently thinks these rocks an eligible station, and from them the captain, as he pulled ashore in his galley, shot a beautiful white spoonbill with a lemon-coloured crest. Geese, ducks and gulls are congregated together here in goodly numbers. The blue rock-pigeon appears to have regularly taken possession of, and to have colonised, "Hai-leu," which is the proper Chinese name of the island. The number and variety of other birds which make it their dwelling-place is remarkable. Swallows build in the caves which are hollowed out in parts of the huge trachyte cliffs, and here and there, on a giant pinnacle, is found a secure eyrie for the eagle and the kite.

In the chasms of the deep precipices, where the sun glints on vast surfaces of shining silvery micaceous schist, on narrow ledges of white gleaming trachyte, and on the black, frowning, weather-stained, lichen-spotted masses which overhang the little bays, are seen blue rock-pigeons, walking about, cooing, bowing to each other, and daintily preening their feathers. One is quietly perched on a slender graceful spray, which waves in the wind from one of the fissures half-way down a perpendicular wall of rock many hundred feet in descent; while others near the top seem to be paying each other polite attentions on green carpets fragrant with the scent of wild blossoming thyme. Hundreds fly out from the side of the cliff on the report of a gun, and after a short excursion return again to the security of their rocky homes. A brown owl maintains her "ancient solitary reign" in the secret recesses. Numbers of pretty hoopoes are flitting about in their peculiar jaunty manner, raising and depressing their crests, and archly coquetting with one another. Large kites and hawks, of which I have observed two species, sail, poised on outspread wings, high above the island; linnets utter their short pleasing notes as they rise in clouds; and a quail is shot in the high grass at the summit.

The little bays which indent the base of the island are paved with smooth rounded pebbles of felspar and transparent quartz, and are peaceful enough to bathe in, but on the weather side the surf thunders against the rough barnacle-clad boulders, and the war of flint and water is incessant.

Above fifty miles west of the point of Shan-tung we observed a narrow harbour, formed by a deep bight of the coast, and which ends in a creek running over a plain, half grassy and half sandy. This was Kala-hai, but it is not marked in the charts. At the entrance we found a fishing party very busy curing cod and skate, soles and sharks. Their boats were hauled up in the sand and their nets spread out to dry, while all hands under a shed, half buried in heaps of fish, were cleaning and salting with true Chinese industry.

As we followed the course of the creek, we found the view bounded seaward by desolate, undulating sand-hills, and landward by green, pleasant slopes and villages buried in trees. On the sward, between the salt-water lagoon and the sand-hills, herds of neat little oxen were grazing placidly.

On the sandy mud of the half-dry lagoon, a little roundabout crab, taken quite by surprise, was seen quickly scuttling into holes, or with great precipitancy hiding himself in the soft sand. In muddy parts, bivalve mollusks, buried in the mud, were throwing up from their syphons little watery jets. On the sand-hills the bustards were walking about like turkeys, feeding on the dry fruit of a plant unknown to me, or pausing suddenly in their confident strut, with head on one side and outstretched neck. Their quick eye soon saw the strangers, and with a short cry they all ran towards each other, and rose in a little flock of from ten to twenty.

'Any particulars concerning ophioid fishes will, I am sure, be welcome; and have I not a right to speak about snake-fishes? Did I not capture, in the middle of the South Atlantic, a fish which, if it had measured fourteen feet instead of fourteen inches, would have created far more astonishment than the Regalecus Jonesii (Newman)? My fish, (Nemichthys scolopacea, Richardson), taken in the towing-net, and even now without a place in the ichthyological system, much more resembled a sea-serpent than Regalecus. It was scaleless and had sharp-pointed teeth, inclined backwards like those of a serpent. The body was ophioid and spotted on the sides; the eye was large and conspicuous; the jaws were very long, the gape was wide; and the back was furnished with a series of rays which extended, crest-like, from the nape to the end of the tail, which had no caudal fin.

There is a figure of it, from my drawing, in the "Zoology of the Samarang." Who shall say it was not the fry of a very formidable spar-snapping sea monster? But my present object is to show that Swainson is in error, when he says of the ribbon-fishes, "These meteoric fishes appear to live in the greatest depths," &c. My experience to the contrary is founded on the silvery hair-tail (Trichiurus lepturus, Linn.), one of the largest of the flattened small-scaled fishes. At Staunton Island, Shan-tung, we obtained large numbers, averaging five feet in length, including the slender caudal filament.

It is common along many other parts of the coasts of Northern China, and in the Korea, when salted and dried, it forms an important item in the diet of the people. It is most delicate eating, and when cut in lengths and fried, makes a very pretty dish. The bones are so few and easy to separate, that even a hungry man may partake of it without fear of being choked. Everywhere it is taken on the surface, at a considerable distance from the land. Off the Regent's Sword, or Liauti-shan Promontory, great numbers of strange-looking craft in the form of rude rafts put boldly out to sea, with long black nets coiled up snugly in the middle, four men working at huge sculls, while the others smoke and chat. The net is paid out in a circle, and when the end is reached, it is turned back and hauled in, securing frequently large numbers of the silvery hair-tail. Many hundreds of these rafts surrounded the ship as she sailed through them in the glow of a glorious sunset.

A few nights before the landing of the allied forces at the Pei-ho an interesting phenomenon was visible, namely, that of mock moons and a double rainbow. A circumstance, moreover, which superstitious Chinamen might also regard as a portent, but which the naturalist would certainly look upon with interest, was a shower of beetles. A black species of Rhizotragus (a sort of chaffer) fell down upon the ships in countless numbers. Our awnings were spread, and the beetles descended continuously all the first watch. Numbers were crushed and trodden into the deck, leaving greasy patches which it required the carpenter's plane to obliterate. They afforded constant excitement to "Belle," a beautiful retriever, who passed the night in chasing and crunching them between her teeth. In the morning heaps of the dead and wounded were swept into corners and under guns. Coal-black lines, following the ripples of the tide, stretched away for miles down the Gulf, formed entirely of the drowned bodies of these insects.

On the Shan-tung side of the Gulf of Pecheli is a remarkable promontory with a flat, sandy neck, and a saddle-head of granite. This from a distance looks like an island, but on a nearer acquaintance its true nature is obvious. The Surf Duck and Saddle Point go together in my mind and refuse to be separated, so you cannot have one without the other. A gale of wind had swept over the Gulf the day previously, and the water was now unsettled and turbid. A dull haze, formed of fine sand, filled the air, and a "mirage" caused everything at a distance to look distorted, and to assume an unreal appearance. As we landed we encountered at first nothing but the glare of the sand. Along the margin of the shallow bay, and in the seaweedy pools left by the receding tide, were countless myriads of lady-birds, drowned, like Pharaoh's host, in the waters of the sea. They had been blown from the opposite coast, and were now driven up by the waves in ridges miles long and in red heaps among the hollows and corners of the outcropping granite rocks. Here and there we came across a magnificent swimming-crab; but these waifs and strays were just as eagerly sought after by lean, hungry cormorants and loud-screaming gulls as by inquisitive peripatetic naturalists, who only came in for a scattered mass of fragments too hard and spiky even for the maw of cormorant and gull.

As we descended the brown and barren stone-strewn hill towards a little Sahara of sand, a hare limped away before us, and the hot bare rocks were enlivened by the coquettish movements of the pretty hoopoe; but beyond these and grasshoppers there were no signs of life. We passed through a small, close, unsavoury village, and arrived at a vast level, sandy plain, quite hard and dry in some parts, but showing generally the characters of a salt-water swamp, with glistening white patches of encrusting salt, shallow lagoons, and tawny spaces where the curlews stalked about like so many diminutive ostriches, and where, by common agreement, avocets, sandpipers, and godwits assembled for a diligent search for palatable worms. Across this weary waste mules and donkeys were wending their way in single file along the narrow paths, and here and there a dark blue dot pointed out some patient Chinaman digging land-crabs for his supper. As we were going off to the ship, the poor fishermen, in great dog-skin boots, came in through the surf, in rude, log-built catamarans. Weary and dripping, they flung down on the sand great heaps of turbot and plaice, soles and skate. They had also brought with them dead surf-ducks in astonishing numbers. These, they said, were drowned in the gale and got foul of their nets. These ducks are not uncommon all along the Shan-tung coast. They are ungainly, surf-loving birds, seeking safety from the sportsman chiefly in diving, and are very difficult to hit. On the flash of the gun they dive under the water, hardly ever waiting for the report. They fly in a straight line just above the surface, in a heavy and awkward manner. As articles of food they are abominable, their flesh being hard, dark, dry, and fishy.

CHAPTER IX.

The Great Wall—Quaint-looking Watch house—Inquisitive Sons of Ham—Visit to the Temples—Birds Shot by our Sportsmen—Hawking at the Great Wall—Flowers and Insects—Wreck of the Medusa—Scarcity of Land Shells—Humming-bird Hawk-moth—The Shield Shrimp—Staunton Island.

As we approached the slightly projecting angle of the coast of Pecheli, where the Great Wall ends in the waters of the Gulf of Liau-tung, we perceived a narrow tawny line of sand and some green clusters of dark trees, with the gable ends of joss-houses showing through the foliage, and for a background a slate-coloured mountain range. The Great Wall, with its square towers and crenellated parapet, climbs the distant hills, and winds along the level plain at their base. Landing at some rocks, we passed through a gap in the ruined pier of the Sea-Gate, mounted a flight of broad granite steps, and got upon the top of the wall. Here we saw a quaint-

VISIT TO TEMPLES. 111

looking watch-house, with high-peaked roof and twisted gables. In and about this building were some fat and lean mandarins, very self-important in appearance, with a few Tartar soldiers, horses and all, and a very inquisitive mass of shaven-pated, narrow-eyed, long-tailed sons of Ham. The "observed of all observers," we passed through the intensely-staring throng, who pressed upon us until our walk upon the Great Wall of China was an accomplished fact.

When we again descended to the sandy plain, we visited the temples seen nestling so prettily in the sacred groves of dark-leaved trees. Here we found ourselves among fantastic gable ends and carvings, gilded dragons, and great bells hung in old-fashioned belfries. In the court-yard of the temple of the biggest Joss was an antique bronze urn, and on either side a colossal tortoise bearing on its back an upright monolith covered with inscriptions. These old stone tortoises are possibly coeval with the Great Wall, and fashioned some 2080 years ago. The surrounding country has, for this part of

China, rather a flourishing aspect, although the buildings within the Sea-Gate are in ruins, and the famous "Myriad-mile Wall," as the Chinese, in the pride of their hearts, love to call it, is in a very dilapidated condition, and in some parts is even banked up, being nearly covered with sand.

Sheaves of newly-cut millet (the common food-plant of North China) were piled up in every field—for it was harvest time at the Great Wall; and scattered over the plain were little straggling homesteads, for the most part snugly embosomed among trees, the flat roofs of the low mud-built houses just visible here and there through the green foliage. A few Chinamen were quietly at work among the millet, and groups of donkeys were reposing in the broad shadow of the Great Wall, which is seen extending in a long line until it seems to vanish in the far distance. Here we halted, while friend Bedwell sketched the scene, and I smoked a pipe and contemplated the novel and interesting landscape from behind the cloud. While we were thus engaged, an old grey-bearded man silently joined us, and solemnly lighted *his* pipe by means of a burning glass (a large pebble lens without a flaw or scratch,) which he mysteriously produced from the folds of his garments.

As we have everywhere observed along the shores of this Gulf, a belt of sandy soil fringes the seaboard, where burdock and the yellow toadflax, a small blue-flowered iris, the wild onion, and the crane's-bill are the only plants, and lizards and grasshoppers the only animals. In some parts the ground is swampy, and there are several shallow snipe-haunted freshwater pools. Here some teal and the Garganey duck were shot by our sportsmen, besides some curlews and a few golden plovers. Two species of heron, the gray and the white, are common; and in this locality the godwit, the snipe, and the sanderling find themselves at home. In the act of demolishing a frog the great bittern was wounded, and rather astonished the dog "Dash," as, with sharp open beak and bristling loose neck-feathers, he fiercely stood at bay. Overhead the wild geese and ducks were flying south in immense flocks before the cold northerly gales. The ubiquitous magpie was, of course, observed perched on the village trees, and the serious rook had work of his own among the grubs in the newly ploughed fields. A golden-crested wren was hopping daintily among the low bushes; the wagtail was jerking about the dry mudflats; the skylark, rising heavenward with his song of praise, was lost among the clouds; and the quail was to be seen everywhere.

Among the crowd of Chinamen at the Great Wall, men are frequently seen with beautiful tame hawks on their wrists. These are goshawks, which they fly at quail. Falconry having come originally from the far East, the practice is doubtless more ancient than the Great Wall itself. In hawking for quail a man is required to carry a net for the captured birds, and also to beat the cover. When a quail rises the master of the hawk directs her attention to the quarry. The goshawk darts forward and seizes the quail in her talons. The man with the net then runs up to her, and takes away the quail, which is deposited with the other captured birds in his net. In this manner as many as twenty brace of quail may be taken in a day. The goshawk has a long silken cord round her neck, which is wound on a reel secured to the arm of her owner.

* * * * *

Fleecy white clouds were sailing softly across the pale blue sky, and a single skylark was singing clear and loud overhead. From the bay on the south side of Cape Vansittart, I passed to the bay on the north side. I reached a sandy down, where many flowers reminded me of home and "merrie England." Among others I observed the storksbill and the toadflax, but not the "wee modest crimson-tipped flower" we all love so well. In its place, however, was the Chinese pink, which grew in abundance everywhere. A pretty campanula was also very common, and springing up in dry stony places were the spikes of a white-flowered stone-crop, looking just like a pigmy aloe in a miniature desert. Grasshoppers leaped up around me in prodigious numbers, and among the stunted shrubs slowly stalked the grass-green mantis. The humming-bird hawk-moth hovered around the spikes of the sedum, and flitting about were painted lady and clouded yellow butterflies.

As we were strolling on, we came to the edge of an abrupt, broken, yellow-fronted cliff, whence issued the harsh, grating song of the tree-cricket, and where, flying backwards and forwards, were many blue rock-pigeons. We descended the cliff, and before us perceived a blue bay with blue hills in the distance. Around us were brown, flat-topped and angular rocks, bristling with black patches of juvenile mussels, and rough with white patches of juvenile barnacles. The ubiquitous Lampaniæ, a kind of sea-screw, were crawling in the little pools, in which also the lively, big-headed gobies and the sly, artful blenny were disporting themselves. Here also, we observed running about, in a busy, cheerful, bustling manner, the beautiful golden plover, the red-billed oystercatcher, the greenshank, and the sanderling.

When we got down to the "lean-ribbed" sand, a

tawny waste was perceived extending right and left for miles; and spotted teal were feeding at the margin of the water. But what is that mysterious object rolling and tumbling in the ripple of the tide? We observe its motions for a short time with a curious eye, but on approaching perceive that it is an immense Rhizostoma, stranded and helpless, at the mercy of the waves. It was certainly the biggest jelly-fish I had ever seen, measuring three feet across the disk. The unfortunate Medusa had not only the misfortune to be wrecked, but had to suffer the still more dire calamity of being eaten. Chinamen came down, like Riff pirates, or Cornish wreckers, to the scene of the disaster, and cut off huge slices of the firm translucent blubber, and carefully wrapping them in cloths carried them away for gastronomic use. Doubtless their insipid mess of boiled rice was greatly improved thereby at evening "chow-chow." This is the only instance I have known of any of the Acalephæ being used as food.

On all the elevated breezy downs—and they are

very numerous along the sea-board of Shan-tung and Liau-tung, and more especially on their exposed and rounded summits, where the soil is scant and stony—hardly anything flourishes but thistles and snails! But none of these snails are half so attractive as the humming-bird hawk-moths, with which these localities are always associated in my mind. The Sedums are in full flower, and cover the surface of the earth with little golden pyramids, magazines of nectar, around which hover the macro-glossæ, the only sentient things, save the snails, one claims acquaintance with on these barren heights, unless, indeed, you cross the highest ridge at the highest point, and look down upon the jagged fractured rocks of black basalt, when you may see the gulls and oystercatchers, and hear their melancholy wail and the harsh cry of the fishing cormorant, mingling with the roar of the great toppling waves as they come thundering in upon the boulders at the base. But in the quiet sunny spots where the Sedums bloom, round and round hover the pretty moths, vibrating their wings and probing with their spiral tongues the yellow pyramids of stars which gladden the dull earth.

The scarcity of land-shells may possibly be owing to the barren granitic nature of the hills, and also to the high state of cultivation of the plains and valleys. On the hills we breathe very pure air, and gaze on picturesque rugged rocks, but see few flowers and no blooming heather; nor does the red sandy loam below reveal the outline of fairy tarn or lakelet. Snails are said to have great partiality for limestone, but here all is granite. The vegetation, moreover, is never varied or luxuriant enough to supply the wants of any great herbivorous snails whose *pabulum vitæ* is leaves. On upland slopes the pale yellow stars of Chrysanthemum chinense may attract the eye, and sometimes a modest violet peeps out from beneath the shelter of a clod, or a dull purple crowfoot is seen, or a little deep blue gentian emerges from the sandy loam. The rest of the vegetation is made up of burdock, wormwood, toadflax, and hawkweed, and the sandy parts are covered with a hard spiky grass.

On the 12th of September we landed on a projecting point, marked on the charts as an island, on the eastern side of the Gulf of Liau-tung, about forty miles north of Hulu-Shan Bay. On leaving the boat near the rocky Cape Vansittart, which is separated from the mainland by a flat sandy neck, we approached a rounded knoll, on the summit of which was a square watch-tower with Tartar horsemen grouped picturesquely around it; a scene my artist friend Bedwell was desirous of sketching. In the distance were the angular cold gray peaks and ridges of a barren mountain range, with here and there little rivers running down their sides, gleaming like quicksilver as the sun shone on the water-courses and little winding streams. At the base of these lifeless granite masses stretched a level plain, green and fertile, where little straggling hamlets of low flat-topped mud houses were snugly sheltered in long groves of trees. To this succeeded a sterile sandy belt, with a chain of freshwater ponds, shallow and full of weeds, and with muddy open spaces between them—the natural resort of the curlew, the whimbrel, the plover, and the snipe. Here, also, we saw the spotted crake, a very sly little fellow, keeping close in the cover of the reeds and grass. The pretty but scentless Chinese pink a little blue-flowered iris, and a yellow, red and white mixture of the blossoms of the tormentil, the heads of sanguisorba, and the loose corymbs of the flower of yarrow, completed nearly all the plants that redeemed the sandy soil from sameness and utter sterility. Nearer the sea long salt-water lagoons and shallow swamps extended, covered in some parts with a white-flowered sea-lavender and the blue stars of Aster Tripolium. From these the great white heron slowly rose, with bright yellow bill pointing out in front, and long black legs stretched out behind, and after a few lazy flaps with his huge curved wings, alighted again to resume his interrupted fishing. Equally familiar was his yet larger cousin in gray, the common heron, and, standing on one leg, her loose snowy plumes waving in the breeze, the elegant white egret dreamed of frogs and fishes. Sandpipers and greenshanks ran piping and probing about the margin, and gulls and little terns screamed, quarrelled, and hovered over the heads both of bipeds and birds.

As I stooped to collect some specimens of pond-snails in one of the clear freshwater ponds with a bottom of sandy mud, my attention was arrested by an object which at first sight I regarded as an unknown genus of bivalve mollusca, but on placing it in a bottle of water the real nature of the creature became revealed. It was an Entomostracon. As a whale among minnows, so, said I, is my new genus among waterfleas; but again I was mistaken. I had not fished long before I brought to light a veritable apus, or shield-shrimp, and I saw at once that my supposed new genus was the young of this creature, thus illustrating very prettily the law in the development of organised beings, that the transition state of a higher form will represent the permanent condition of genera lower in the scale of being. I cannot find any account of the metamorphoses of the Apodidæ, or whether it is known that in the young state the shield is folded on itself longitudinally in the form of a bivalve shell which entirely conceals the head, body, and feet of the animal. There is but a single large black eye in these young ones, situated Polyphemus-like in the middle of the forehead. The very young larvæ are of a pale horn colour, and swim in a steady manner forwards, the ventral edge of the shell being directed downwards. As they move through the water they partially expand and close the valves of the shell. Older and larger individuals are olivaceous, and are fond of lying on their sides in the sand at the edge of the pond, now and then spinning round and round by means of their protruded tail. The adult of Kroyer's shield-shrimp, as it may be called, keeps in deep water, and is voracious and predatory, not confining his attention to small things in the water, but even feeding on drowned dragon-flies.

* * * * *

The little island called Staunton Island, near the Shan-tung promontory, is very high and rocky, with an irregular green summit. Iron-bound and inaccessible, one little cove alone serves as a landing place, above which, clustering together in every accessible ledge, are fishermen's huts, looking, when seen from a distance, like a group of martins' nests. On landing, we mounted from one stony terrace to another by rude steps cut in the rock, and saw around us and above us nothing but fish —fish in various forms, but chiefly split open, and drying on the great bare rocks.

The blue pigeon has possession of the wall-faced cliffs, and feeds unmolested in the hollows of their grassy tops. Here also a pretty blue thrush flies from one lichen-spotted boulder to another; and now and then the great brown lizard, a species of skink, emerges from his hiding place in the crevice of some rock.

CHAPTER X.

The Korea—Among the Islands—Odd Names of Mountain Peaks—Victoria Harbour—Beacon Fires—Visit from the Natives—Their Picturesque Appearance—Description of the Chief—Costume of the Natives—Worship of Bacchus—Their Rude Manners—Their Curiosity—Modes of Salutation—An Anecdote.

LEAVING the huge cone-like island of Quelpart in the distance, the freshening breeze bears us gallantly along towards those unknown islands which form the Archipelago of Korea. As you approach them you look from the deck of the vessel and you see them dotting the wide blue boundless plain of the sea— groups and clusters of islands stretching away into the far distance. Far as the eye can reach, although that is not many miles, their dark masses can be faintly discerned, and, as we close, one after another the bold outlines of their mountain peaks stand out clearly against the cloudless sky. The water, from which they seem to arise, is so deep around them that a ship can almost range up alongside them. The rough grey granite and bare basaltic cliffs of which they are composed, show them to be only the rugged peaks of submerged mountain-masses, which have been rent in some great convulsion of nature from the peninsula which stretches into the sea from the mainland. You gaze upward and see the weird fantastic outline which some of their torn and riven peaks present. In fact, they have assumed such peculiar forms as to have suggested to navigators characteristic names. Here, for example, stands out the fretted, crumbling towers of one called "Windsor Castle;" there frowns a noble rock-ruin, the "Monastery;" and here again, mounting to the skies, is "Abbey Peak."

I was reading the other day some travels, by an old author, in Mongolia, and was struck by the suggestive names which the Tartars have seized upon to designate the remarkable features of some of *their* mountain peaks; where, instead of " Windsor Castle" we have the " Five-ugly-Devils," and instead of " Abbey Peak" the " Five-horses'-heads."

Some of the islands of this Archipelago are very lofty, and one was ascertained to boast of a naked granite peak more than two thousand feet above the level of the sea. Many of the summits are crowned with a dense forest of conifers, dark trees very similar in appearance to Scotch firs.

After several days spent among these islands, we sailed one evening, very tranquilly, into the wide deep bay which has received the name in English charts of Victoria Harbour, but which is known to the natives as Tsau-lian, situated on the mainland of Korea, and which forms the southern boundary of Manchuria. Captain Broughton, who first discovered it, gave it the name of Tcho-San, most probably from hearing the natives call all the surrounding country O-tchu-San. As we came to an anchor, in the dusk of the evening, beacon fires burst forth on all the neighbouring hills, a sure sign of the watchfulness, if not alarm, of the jealous people we were come to visit.

Betimes on the next day, large, heavy, flat-bottomed boats came off from the nearest land, pulling slowly, but steadily, towards the ship, and filled with the rabble of a chief, who occupied the largest boat. A flourish of trumpets, or rather conches, announced his approach, and when he stepped on board he was saluted with three guns. The boatmen were rough, brawny fellows, with coarse Tartar features, bronzed by exposure to the weather, with unkempt hair, shaggy beards, and uncouth bearing. They could not be persuaded by the most vociferous upbraidings, not even by threats of the bastinado, to mind their boats, but would throng on board with the chief and his followers, and gaze upon the "Devils of the Western Sea,"—and soon a motley group formed on the deck.

The chief, who really had something very noble and majestic about him, as is generally the case with men in high authority among the natives of those islands, was duly presented, and seated himself upon a mat placed for him by one of his attendants. The demeanour of those of his countrymen who surrounded him was as free and independent as his own was reserved and dignified. With their strange costumes, easy movements, and the animation of their manner excited by curiosity, the entire group presented a very picturesque appearance.

The aspect of the old man, with his grey flowing beard, bushy eyebrows, solemn visage, and mild observant eyes, was very imposing. In his hand he held his badge of office, a wand of ebony with a green silken cord entwined about it like the serpent of Æsculapius. Two pages stood behind him with his fan, tobacco pouch, and umbrella, his long-stemmed pipe being in his own hand. He was dressed in a loose violet-coloured robe, with the cuffs of the sleeves turned up with scarlet, which covered, and partly concealed, an inner crimson tunic reaching below the knees. His loose, wide pantaloons of green were tied in above his ankles, and on his feet he wore white socks and black leather boots, much pointed and turned up at the toes, resembling those worn by the courtiers in the reign of Charles the Second. His venerable head was protected by the broad-brimmed, high-crowned hat of black-stained bamboo network, a hat peculiar, I imagine, to the people of this remarkable country.

Grouped around this central figure were a few soldiers, with tails of red horse-hair depending from their hats, and armed with short swords. A few other men about him had rather an air of superiority to the others. These were distinguished by a single peacock's feather attached to the apex of the pointed crown of their hats, and hanging down gracefully over the extensive brim. Peacocks being unknown in the Korea, these feathers, as is the case among the Chinese, are brought, no doubt, as tribute from India, and have been bestowed upon those by whom they are worn, as marks of distinction, by their king. It is as a similar mark of distinction that the Emperor of China presents a peacock's feather to such of his higher functionaries as he desires to reward with some emblem of his especial favour.

The costume of the poorer people is still the same as I find it described in the most complete account of Korea to which I have had access, namely, that of Hamel, who has given us the "Travels of some Dutchmen in Korea." The only references, however, in his work to the dress of these singular people are very brief, though sufficiently characteristic. "These men," he says, "are clad after the Chinese fashion, excepting only their hats, which are of horsehair;" and again, "The poorer sort have no clothes but what are made of hemp and pitiful skins."

The serfs, or Coolies, as we may term them, don a loose wide jacket of a coarse cotton material, tied across the chest, in a somewhat slovenly manner, by a string. This jacket, which reaches as far as the waist, is furnished with short, wide sleeves. The lower portions of their bodies are protected by short, wide trowsers, reaching down to just above the knee, their legs and feet being bare. Their hats, when they have any, are large slouching sombreros, made of brown felt. Many men whom I saw striding in from the villages, with long staves like alpenstocks in their hands, were clothed in thick, padded coats, and had on their heads shaggy conical caps of fur. These specimens of the rural population, I also observed, were stalwart-looking fellows, several of them being of more than usually large proportions.

We did not encourage the visits of these people, who, if not restrained, would have come on board at all hours, and quite overrun the ship. They were by no means welcome or agreeable visitors, for the plain fact must be stated that they were somewhat unsavoury and not over clean. They were like those Tartars mentioned in an old book of travels by William de Rubruquis—"They never wash any cloaths—nay, they beat such as wash, and take their garments from them!" Moreover, they pilfer when they can. A sort of grandee was regaling himself in our ward-room with a cheery glass, when the steward, ever watchful in his pantry, spied one of his attendant pages adroitly pocketing a spoon. Kleptomaniacs, thought I, in this country should be more careful, for I read in Hamel that "punishment for theft in the Korea is to be trampled to death!" In this particular case, however, the culprit was threatened and soundly abused by the bacchanalian grandee, his master, and turned out of the ship by the captain.

As a nation, I am sadly afraid these people are greatly addicted to the worship of Bacchus. During my small excursions on shore I witnessed many an old serf inebriated with samshoo; and I often saw groups, quite worthy of Cruikshank's famous picture, crowding round mighty jars of a sort of fermented liquor like beer. These men evidently loved the beverage as much as even jovial Jack Falstaff, and, like the boors in Tennant's "Anster Fair," they—

"Grow by boosing boisterously merry."

Moreover, they do not seem to have improved in this respect since the time when Hamel was among them in 1653. Being then presented with the captain's cup (who was drowned when the ship went ashore,) and with a pot of red wine saved from the wreck, that traveller says, "They liked the liquor so well that they drank till they were very merry."

One trait in their character, which is far from recommending them to strangers visiting their shores, is their extreme rudeness. On more than one occasion, my gentle-mannered companion, a little man with roundish eyes, and myself, whose nose is not a snub, were surrounded by a rough but not unfriendly mob, who treated us in a most unceremonious manner. Our personal peculiarities seemed to afford them much amusement, reminding us of a passage in Huc's China, when the tall man Huc, and the short man Gabet, were, at Yao-tchang, submitted to a similar scrutiny. One of these inquisitive critics remarked, "The little devil has very large eyes, and the tall one a very pointed nose." In a similar way our hair and skin were freely commented upon; the fineness of the one and the smoothness of the other being greatly admired. Our persons and garments were subjected to the most minute examination, conducted in a manner at once familiar and rude. The fashion and texture of our clothes were made the subject of endless observations. Our gilt buttons were greatly admired, and to all appearance ardently coveted. Even the contents of our pockets were turned out, passed from hand to hand, and freely criticised, but, be it said to their credit, always honestly restored to their legitimate owners.

When we were many years ago among the gentle and inoffensive Loo Chooans, we were often surrounded by a crowd of eager gazers, all gaping upon us with looks of concentrated curiosity; but among that peaceful race the Book of Rites is respected, and the "hundred families," as the Chinese term the people, looked upon us at a respectful distance: the children placed in the front ranks, the next rank kneeling, and the tall ones standing in the rear; but we experienced no treatment like that to which we were subjected here, where we were made the butt of the rabble, who never seemed to weary of the amusement which they derived from the inspection of our peculiarities, national and personal. While we were surrounded by these uncouth gentry, we could not fail to be reminded, moreover, of the contrast between their rude manners and the graceful salutations of the polished Japanese; or between their vulgar and obtrusive curiosity, and the polite forms of the people of the Flowery Land. These Koreans seem to have no idea of a generous and refined hospitality to strangers. Towards us individually they did not show a single mark of respect, and treated us with but scant courtesy. Their treatment of us did not proceed from ignorance, for they have a code of etiquette which is strictly followed among themselves, the poorer classes prostrating themselves before their superiors.

Most races of men have some peculiar mode of salutation, some of them, to us, apparently highly original. The Tartars scratch their ears and put out their tongues; a custom which affords M. Huc an occasion for one of his delicate strokes of humour. That adventurous missionary, finishing the account of his interview with the chief of the police at La-Ssa, in which he was accompanied by

M. Gabet, says, "After politely putting out our tongues we withdrew." There are, however, modes of salutation even more ludicrous than this. Some savages, the name of whose tribe I forget, when they wish to show their respect, roll on their backs, kick up their legs, and slap repeatedly the outside of their thighs. The chief of the Ahts, of Vancouver's Island, when he wishes to pay his neighbour a compliment, puts on a mask stuck full of porcupine's quills, upon which he heaps a quantity of swans' down, and dancing up to his visitor gives a jerk with his head and sends the down all over him. The Wanyamuezi, a tribe in Africa, when they meet each other clap their hands twice; and if a Watusi man meets a woman of the same tribe, she allows her arms to fall by her side while he gently presses her arms below the shoulder. We all have heard, too, of the ceremony of Ongi, or pressing noses, which is the Maori etiquette in New Zealand.

CHAPTER XI.

Exciting Incident—Korean Tombs—Mode of Burial—Dwellings in the Korea—Japanese Outpost—An Entertainment—Hamel's "Travels"—Language of the Koreans—A Commendable Custom—Religious Belief—Priests and Nuns.

DURING our sojourn at Tsaulian an incident occurred which might have been attended with serious consequences. It was considered necessary, for the benefit of future navigators, to fix more correctly the position of this place. The captain, protected by a guard of marines, landed in the morning, and advanced a little way towards a hillock in the immediate vicinity of the large walled town. He was looking about for some favourable spot on which to make his observations, when a party of the natives, who had been silently but jealously watching our every movement, suddenly advanced upon us, thinking, perhaps, we were about to attack their town. One or two of them, armed with old matchlocks and others with sticks, advanced against us, while one, more daring than the rest, closing with the sergeant, attempted to wrest his rifle from him. The captain, however, came briskly to the rescue, and dealt a well-directed blow with his walking-stick upon the knuckles of the assailant, who beat at once a hasty retreat, discomfited and crestfallen. This well-timed action excited the laughter of his would-be-bellicose compatriots, who halted and remained gazing upon us from a safe distance; until, having completed our observations, we packed up our instruments, and, greatly to the relief of the natives, returned to the ship. Mr. Macleod, in his "Voyage of the Alceste," relates an incident very similar, which occurred to the officers of his ship in 1816, and probably at the same place.

The spot from which we made our observation was close upon the confines of their cemetery, and strolling in that direction, I meditated among their tombs. There was, however, not much to foster meditation among the monuments, which for the most part consisted of tall square columns, surmounted by the square effigy of a human head, with a square kind of cap on the top of it. In other tombstones the human form was rendered even less divine, consisting of a rudely sculptured stone image, with a very flat nose, a very wide mouth, and very little oblique eyes, stuck upon a very long neck, stretched out as if the ghost of the defunct were striving to emerge from the long coarse grass of the burial ground. One monument, however, was of considerably higher pretension than the others, the broad headstone being inscribed with the name and position of the deceased in Chinese characters. The tomb was covered with a large square granite slab, and in front of the grave was what appeared to be the model of a little temple or mausoleum.

Hamel, almost the only authority in matters concerning the inner or domestic life of the Koreans, says that "they enclose every corpse in two coffins two or three fingers thick, put one between the other to keep out the water, painting and adorning them according to their ability. Three

DWELLINGS IN THE KOREA.   141

days after the funeral," he adds, "the friends of the dead man return to the grave, where they make some offerings, and then eating all together, are very merry." This funereal feast would seem to resemble an Irish wake, the only difference being that it is a little deferred.

The dwellings of the humbler classes in the Korea are grouped in hamlets, and their tall conical roofs, beneath which are their granaries or store-rooms, are usually thatched with reeds. Each house is separated from its neighbour, and is inclosed within a high stone wall, which entirely conceals from those who might be curious enough to observe them the domestic arrangements of the inmates. Their villages, when viewed from a distance, present somewhat the appearance of the dwellings of those white ants whose communities near Senegal are so well described by Adanson.

In the cities and large walled towns, the roofs of the houses are covered with tiles, and the floors of the rooms are hollow underneath. In these hollows fires are kindled to warm the inmates in winter. The richer inhabitants have gardens and courtyards ornamented with fish-ponds, and planted with dwarfed trees in the Japanese style.

In a quiet stroll I came across a stone-built cabin, a sort of isolated cottage placed in a little garden. Not a soul was visible, so I entered cautiously and peered about. It was a long narrow house, with two pointed gable-ends, and a sloping roof, which projected into wide eaves, forming a balcony, supported by stout wooden posts, under the shade of which a long raised bench or platform extended the whole length of the building. On this platform I pictured the entire family sitting cross-legged on a long summer's day, smoking, chatting, and laughing at some good joke. The windows were square, and instead of glass were covered with oiled paper; they were furnished, moreover, with moveable wooden shutters. I entered the cooking room, and found it a very dirty, dingy, low, unsavoury kitchen, with a bench at the further end, elevated a little above the floor, whereon stood the cooking utensils belonging to the household, a huge earthen water jar, and sundry wooden bowls! The "superintendent of the cauldron," as they term the cook in China, cannot, I think, be required to exercise much culinary talent in devising the list of dishes for the table. In this poor household, I ventured to predict they were summed up in one simple word—Porridge!

The food of the Koreans generally is of no great variety, and their dishes are very simple in their composition. The more wealthy and substantial among them have condiments with their boiled rice, and with their chopsticks help themselves to tit-bits of savoury pork and boiled fowl; but the poorer classes are obliged to content themselves with less generous fare, barley-meal and the coarse flour prepared by pounding millet being the principal means of sustaining life. Rice will grow only in the southern portion of the peninsula.

At one period of their history the Koreans occupied a considerable portion of Eastern Tartary, from which, however, they were driven out, and obliged to take refuge in the peninsula which now bears their name. Old Hamel mentions, that when he was at Sior (which, he says, is the name of the capital), a Tartar envoy arrived demanding the usual tribute, on which occasion he and his shipwrecked companions were sent away to a great fort till the ambassador had departed, the king fearing that their detention in the hands of the Koreans would come to the ears of the great Khan.

They have also been conquered by the Japanese. In the heroic times of the Mikados, the Empress Yengon sent an expedition for the subjugation of the Korea, which was completely successful. The country was again invaded by the Mongols, when the Siogoun Yoritomo defeated Kublai Khan. The victors in these expeditions carried off much valuable booty, which is exhibited at certain seasons of the year.

On our arrival at Victoria Harbour, we saw the national flag of Japan waving from the flagstaff of an ornamental red-tiled house, most pleasantly situated in a grove of trees. This we found, on inquiry, was an outpost of Japan, and occupied by a mandarin of some rank, and a guard of soldiers. When Hamel was a prisoner among the Koreans, in 1653, he says, alluding to their then crippled state, "Now both Tartars and Chinese tyrannise over them."

I accompanied the captain in his galley, to call upon the Japanese officer, but on entering a small camber near their settlement, we were met by numbers of sharp-prowed boats, which attempted to bar our further progress; upon which, the crew were told to arm themselves with the boat's stretchers, and bring those who were opposing our progress to order. Our men, accordingly, obedient to command, dealt about them pretty lustily, and the Japanese soon giving way, we effected a landing. We had not yet, however, gained our object, for, on arriving at the entrance of their stronghold, we were decidedly shut out, and on demanding admittance it was peremptorily denied. So we proceeded on board again, and despatched the interpreter to demand an explanation, with the threat of the alternative of a bombardment early next morning!

This decided treatment seemed to bring them at once to their senses, for the interpreter brought back from the Japanese authorities an invitation to the officers to come on shore and dine with them.

We, of course, accepted the invitation, and at the appointed time made our appearance in epaulettes and side-arms. We were conducted to a handsome lofty hall of audience, where the Great Man sat in state, with a page holding a drawn sword on either side of him. On the same elevated daïs sat two other officials of lower rank. They begged us to be seated, and when we had complied with their request, some young men appeared with little tables and cups of saki, which they placed before us. We all soon became very sociable together, and were on the best terms with our entertainers. The Esha, or doctor of the establishment, was particularly attentive to me. He insisted on presenting me with the medicine box which he usually carried about him, and which, on examination, I saw contained some of those wonderful musk-scented red pills which the Chinese style "supernatural treasure for all desires," and which are supposed to be a true universal panacea for all diseases. The composition of these celebrated pills, like that so highly lauded by the admirers of Old Parr, is a secret in the possession of a single family, and has been faithfully transmitted from generation to generation. I regret to have to observe that my learned brother, towards the latter end of the banquet, got so inebriated that he was reprimanded, and ordered out of the room by the dignified chief. He was a good-looking fellow, closely shaven like a Bonze.

We partook of the sweets and cakes, and other dainties provided for us; but were I to enumerate all the good things with which the tables groaned, I might lay myself open to the imputation of plagiarism — as did the officers of a European Embassy who favoured their readers with a description of a repast which had been given them by the mandarins. This description, however, they had merely copied from the narrative of some Jesuit missionaries who had "written an account more than a hundred years back of a similar entertainment, the dinner being composed of the very same dishes, and served in precisely the same manner." We smoked a good deal, and quaffed many little cups of warm scented pink saki; eventually taking our leave, much pleased with the hospitality shown us. The whole affair reminded us of a similar entertainment very elaborately described by Kempfer, even to the circumstance of the inebriate doctor:—" Good liquor was drunk about plentifully all the while, and the Commissioner's surgeon, who was to treat us, did not miss to take his full dose."

The Editor of Hamel's Travels seems to throw some doubt upon the authenticity of his account, though on very insufficient grounds. The names of the towns through which the shipwrecked Dutchmen passed on their way from the coast to the capital, do not, it appears, correspond with those in a map of the Korea, which they copied from one hung up in the king's palace. The difference, however, may be easily accounted for; the names in the map being doubtless written in Chinese characters, which are entirely different from those employed by the Koreans, a circumstance which might easily lead to some discrepancy.

Hamel himself, in reference to the writing of this people, observes, "They (the Koreans) use three sorts of writing, the first like that of China and Japan, which they use for printing their books, and all public affairs; the second like the common writing among Europeans—the great men and governors use it to answer petitions, and make notes on letters of advice, or the like—the commonalty cannot read this writing; the third is more unpolished, and serves women and the common sort."

The Dutchman resided thirteen years in Korea, some of which time was passed in the capital. Two hundred years ago his ship was wrecked on the Island of Quelpart, having been overtaken by a violent tempest, which "shook their boltsprit, and endangered their prow." They were then overwhelmed by a great wave, which caused the master to cry out "to cut down the mast by the board, and go to their prayers." His account of the appearance, manners, and customs of the Koreans faithfully represents them as they exist at the present day. Their rough appearance and manners have remained unaltered since 1653, for the poor shipwrecked Dutchmen at first were afraid of them:—"Their very habit increased our fear, for it had somewhat frightful, which is not seen in China and Japan." On a longer acquaintance, however, they found them kinder than was warranted by their looks. "We may affirm," says Hamel, "we were better treated by that idolator (the king) than we should have been among Christians." Their hatred of foreign interference, and their inhospitable attempts to oppose the landing of strangers, or to hold any communication with them, also remain unaltered since his time. He relates that, in order to incite in their women and children a wholesome dread of his poor countrymen, they spread a report that they "were of a monstrous race, and when they drank were obliged to tuck up their noses behind their ears."

One custom which prevails among them is worthy of imitation even by the most advanced of

Christian nations, and that is the care which the sons take of the old people. "When a father," says Hamel, "is fourscore years of age, he declares himself incapable of managing his estate, and resigns it up to his children. Then the eldest, taking possession, builds a house at the common expense for his father and mother, where he lodges and maintains them with the greatest respect." How often is this sacred duty imperfectly fulfilled, or even entirely neglected, among ourselves!

The Koreans, in the time of Hamel, seem to have indulged in some latitudinarianism with regard to religious faith and practice, for we read that "the common people make odd grimaces before the idols, but pay them little respect; and the great ones honour them much less, because they think themselves to be more than an idol." The doctrine of Calvin evidently does not find favour among them; their opinion being that good doers shall be rewarded, and evil doers be punished. Their priests appear to be followers of Buddha. "They shave their heads and beards, must eat nothing that had life, and are forbidden conversing with women." As among some other communities besides Korean, some of the priests "go a-begging," but the greater number, a circumstance which is rare among any other communities, "work for their living, or follow some trade." They are haunted by some vague traditionary idea of the Tower of Babel, believing, says our old Dutchman, that "mankind originally only had one language, but that the design of building a tower to go up to heaven caused the confusion of tongues." They have numerous convents or nunneries, where live societies of religious women, who are "all shorn, abstain from flesh, serve idols, and may not marry." Kempfer, in his History of Japan, also mentions "a certain remarkable religious order of young girls called Birkuni, or nuns, which damsels," he informs us, obtain their living by begging, and are, in his opinion, "the handsomest girls we saw in Japan."

CHAPTER XII.

Port of Mah-lu-san—A Seining Party—Beautiful Scene—Hauling the Seine—A Viviparous Fish—Encounter with a Snake—A Clever Thief—Deer Island—Buck Shooting—Lichens and Toads—The Sunny Gorge—Wilford's Rest—Range of the Tiger.

ONE afternoon, while lying at anchor in the safe and pretty port of Mah-lu-san, one of the Korean group, there was a seining party, which I accompanied. The day was lovely; the whole face of the country was bright and smiling; the barley was ripe in the fields, the hills were covered with a varied green, and the little rippling waves of the clear water of the bay were dancing in the sun. Stretching far away to the north and to the south were groups of dark-blue islets, rising mistily from the surface of the sea—glimpses of that mysterious archipelago among the unknown islands of which I cruised in by-gone years. The sea was covered with large picturesque boats, which, crowded with Koreans in their white fluttering robes, were putting off from the adjacent villages, and sculling across the pellucid water to visit the stranger ship.

We chose a sheltered bay, and commenced paying out the seine. Koreans, seated in groups, bare-headed, or wearing their broad-brimmed hats, were smoking their pipes in silence, as they inquisitively observed our proceedings. The rooks in the tall and glorious trees that fringed the bay cawed loudly with indignant remonstrance at the unwonted intrusion upon their quiet haunts; while the sailors, to the tune of their popular songs, hauled in the great net, in which upwards of one hundred and seventy pounds of bream and other fish were taken.

I, of course, took the opportunity while here of pursuing, with my usual zeal, my natural-history inquiries. Among the denizens of the sea I noticed toad-fishes, devil-fishes, sea-horses, and swimming-crabs. I also noticed a great many individuals of a singular viviparous fish, most of which had three or four living young ones in their bellies. I believe the fish belongs to a genus described by Temminck under the name of Ditrema. I also found, as I strolled away from the seining party, a singular species of Arum, with long curling horns extending from its lurid spathes. The natives were just as friendly as when I visited the group in 1845. An old man with a basket of sea-weed on his back stopped me, and would fain persuade me to taste of his Laminarian dainty. A little further on, a young lad made a friendly advance by biting off a portion of lily root and offering me the remainder; while a small boy brought me wild raspberries strung upon a straw.

On one occasion, while out with my friend Buckley in search of adventures, we observed a sandy mud-flat in the distance, on the other side of which was a breakwater formed of heaped-up boulders. On approaching nearer, we were struck with a peculiar blue appearance of the sand-flat; which, strange to say, on our arrival suddenly disappeared, but not before the cause of the peculiar phenomenon revealed itself in the form of thousands of struggling, round-bodied, blue crabs, which were frantically endeavouring to hide themselves in the yielding sand, for such is the remarkable habit of Scopimera globosa. The wave-worn stones of the breakwater were partly concealed by tangled vines, and the creeping stems of Convolvulus maritima. On this occasion we had to do battle with a snake. While Buckley was proceeding in advance, I observed that he suddenly became excited, stopped, and beckoned, pointing emphatically right before him. Sure that something must be wrong, I hurriedly rushed to his assistance, just in time to cut off the retreat of a large mottled snake as he was trying to escape among the tangled vines and boulders. A slight blow on the back arrested his progress, paralysing the after-part of the body. He turned fiercely round, hissing, and protruding his long, black, fork-like tongue. We both belaboured the unfortunate reptile, and soon finished him. An examination of his mouth showed him to be a snake of a highly venomous character, the poison-fangs being truly formidable.

The day was oppressive, and we soon began to suffer from the heat, but the sight of a lonely hut not far off suggested the promise of water to assuage our thirst. On approaching the house to prefer our modest request, we were startled at the apparition of an old woman, fierce and angry, brandishing a big stick. As she advanced rapidly upon us, she seemed in such a fury that to avoid the outburst of her rage we ignominiously turned and fled, amid a volley of what was indubitably Korean Billingsgate.

When at a safe distance, we sat pensively on the lonely rocks, and, to soothe our ruffled spirits, smoked a pipe, at the same time watching the movements of a boy gathering barnacles. With a sharp stone he deftly detached them from the surface of the rock, picked out the fish, deposited them in a large oyster-shell, and then, leaving his gathered store, wandered on in search of more.

Having nothing better to do, we speculated as to who he was. Was he the old crone's grandson? Were the barnacles for bait, or were they for supper? We soon remarked that we were not the only clever ones who watched the boy. A solitary rook followed his motions with a knowing eye, and when he saw him at a safe distance, pounced softly on the tempting morsels, gobbled them up greedily, and, with a mocking caw of exulting defiance, winged his way to the distant trees.

Forming one side of Chusan Harbour in the Korea is a green hilly island, called "Deer Island," covered with low trees, chiefly dwarf scrub, and full of loose, moss-grown, lichen-covered stones. In some parts the sides of the hills are furrowed by water-courses, where the wild pig feeds on the fallen acorns, and where the little hog-deer comes to drink. In other parts, the broad base of the hill expands into grassy plains, where troops of horses graze, and where we found scattered ponds, rush-bordered, the favourite resort of shy, sober-plumaged widgeons and little rounded, bright-eyed teal. In one of the deep-shaded, thickly-wooded ravines of this charming island, I captured one of my famous beetles, named by Pascoe in my honour, Dicranocephalus Adamsi!

I was ashore, as was my custom, with the "merrie men" of the watering party, and, as was also my wont, on the alert for specimens. Net in hand, I wandered over the glorious hill-side, beating now and then the dense cover of oak-scrub for leaf-rolling snout-beetles and the long-nosed acorn-beetles, or bagging pretty long-horns, as they came flying steadily by. Occasionally I captured glittering gold-beaters and pretty lily-beetles, as they alighted on the sunny leaves in the fern, among the green young oaks. As I wandered on I kept a sharp look out, or, as they say in nautical phrase, I "kept my weather-eye lifting." Friend B., who started with me, having a *penchant* for larger game, and looking down somewhat disdainfully on beetles and such "small deer," had diverged, and, gun in hand, was on the trail of a buck. On a sudden I was made aware that something of an unwonted nature had succeeded in astonishing the mind of my predatory companion, for I heard his voice making the gully resound with the cry, "Doctor, doctor!" Hastening as fast as untractable boughs and the prickly vines of Smilax would allow me, to the scene of his excitement, I was agreeably surprised on beholding a strange, great, and beautiful Coleopteran, feebly struggling in a green bed of oak-leaves, and my friend of the fowling-piece gazing with surprise, not unmixed with alarm, at its unwonted aspect. I knew him for a Goliath, and raised him carefully from his verdurous couch. He had been flying in the sun round a cluster of fir-trees, near the top of the hill, and had fallen, like Icarus of old, from his high estate. His body was covered with a downy bloom, like the sunny side of a ripe plum, and his head was adorned with two conical horns, whence his name, Dicranocephalus, or, "he of the double helmet." He was very strong, and resembled Cetonia and Melolontha. I read in "Maunder" that one specimen, now in the British Museum, was taken on the Himalayan mountains, so that my prize, if not indigenous to the Korea, must have travelled a pretty long way.

The ancient weather-stained masses are often heaped up in the strangest confusion, and possess a positive though borrowed beauty from the Lepralias and other lichens with which they are encrusted. They are usually of a frosty-white, pale-green, or rusty-brown; but sometimes you observe a bright orange patch. Among these lichen-covered fragments of primeval granite I found my "harlequin" toads; and as the rain had brought out the worms and other dainties on which they feed, they were hopping lazily about in all directions. I know not if this very peculiar toad has been described, but I have preserved some specimens in spirit for Dr. Gray. The orange, however, has turned dull yellow from the action of the alcohol.

After much scrambling and unwonted exertion, I found myself on the top of the hill, among a heap of old-world stones. It was just after a heavy rain, and the rocks were still wet and dripping. I saw nothing but a number of these gorgeous toads, in a bright livery of black and scarlet, and lichens enough to have satisfied the desires of the Rev. C. Berkeley himself. The rocks at these elevated situations are larger, and more visible than those below, which, moreover, are often concealed by Eleagnus-bushes, besides Smilax-vines and other creepers.

In the same harbour of Tsau-li-an is a long, high island, familiarly known by us under the name of Deer Island, although its proper appellation is Tsi-kiung-tau. On this island there is a species of deer, a kind of Moschus, the size of a sheep, the male of which is without antlers, and the mouth, in the upper jaw, is armed with very long, sharp-edged, curved, canine teeth. They keep very close under cover, and when driven from the shelter of the dense underwood, bound wildly along, and may then be shot like hares. The lower part of their haunt is shared by half-wild horses, which go in large troops, snorting, prancing, and neighing, or suddenly halting, and having a good long stare at the intruders on their domain. In the level, grassy plains, there are ponds frequented by teal, ducks, frogs, and water-beetles. The mountain-springs form little trickling rivulets, sometimes heard murmuring in subterranean channels under your feet. The Centaurea, and the bird's-foot trefoil, the willow, the iris, and the pink, grow in abundance. The humble-bees wander, droning over the tops of the flowers. I captured three or four species of snout-beetles, one with an egregiously long neck. I beat Balanus from the young oaks, and a cryptorhynchus from the Eleagnus-bushes. Melasoma is common on the willows, and two species of Euchlora on the trailing Smilax. The Apollo ·butterfly and the swallow-tail here sun their gorgeous wings. There are a few rude huts, and, perchance, a solitary woman, in the universal white Korean garments, may be seen pounding millet near the low doorway, while the husband smokes his pipe on the threshold. Higher up, you come to huge stones and masses of rock, all grey, and green, and yellow with lichens, and with Eleagnus-bushes growing up between them. From this you gradually make your toilsome way to Wilford's Rest, where our weary botanist reposed awhile, after gaining the summit of the island. Here, among stubborn, thorny Smilax, and dwarf oak, forming a short, dense scrub, and great loose stones, are the peculiar fastnesses of the deer. Without dogs, you would imagine they were quite unapproachable. However, no less than nine deer fell before the ardour, skill, and patience of my messmates. Sutherland, untiring and sagacious, slew two fat bucks, after toiling and moiling all the livelong day, and gazed on their lifeless forms with a smile of grim satisfaction. A beetle-hunting doctor, in a quiet, bosky dell, was startled by loud shouts from the hill-side, high up among the Smilax-vines and oak-scrub, and, looking up, perceived Warren wildly flourishing a bloody knife. He was shouting in triumph that with his own hand he had brought down his deer and had cut its throat. Down a crooked, stony path Wilford, panting under the carcase of a fine buck, was advancing, staggering but elated; while Schuckburgh came jauntily in, with a young doe slung across his shoulders, and

flung it down as if he had been accustomed to
that sort of thing from his infancy!

* * * * *

Near the shore a shallow creek leaves the mud-flats
dry on the fall of the tide; and here the Korean
boys capture the Razorfish in the same manner as
they do in the North of Scotland. They know by
a sudden little jet of water from the holes in the
sand that the mollusk is at home, and pass down a
stick, with a jagged iron barb at the end, between
the valves of the shell, which close immediately,
and the animal is hauled up.

I found the remains of the tiger both at the
Korea and at Vladimir, showing that the range of
this handsome mammal is much more extended
than is generally believed. Mr. Atkinson says it
has been killed in Siberia, having crossed from the
Kirghis Steppe into the Altai mountains. "The
Kirghis say that wherever the wild boars are
numerous, there the tiger takes up his abode, as
he is fond of pork." Our Manchurian skins are
warmer, and more woolly than those from India.

In the province of Liau-tung they appear to be tolerably abundant, the skins we purchased in the Liao-ho being cheap. The Manchu Tartars in this region dig a deep wide ditch, of a circular form, leaving a little island, as it were, in the centre, on which a man takes up his position. The ditch is then covered over artfully with light brushwood, and the Tiger, spying the man in the middle, makes a spring, and falling short, is speared or shot by hunters on the look-out. In the Korea, the skins seem to be much valued, being reserved for the chiefs. We frequently observed them in the boats of the great men who came alongside.

CHAPTER XIII.

Russian Manchuria—The Coast Line—The Conquerors of China—Tartar Bravery—Province of Liao-tung—Dangerous Navigation—Mouth of the Liao-ho—A Land of Pigs—Use of Cotton Seeds—Furriers Shops—Food Plants of Manchuria—Chinese Influence—Dagelet Island—Sea Bears—Bay of Sio-wu hu—Manchurian Bulls—The Manchus.

HAD Russia not cast a covetous eye upon Manchuria we should not have known much about that fertile tract of land, abounding in gold and silk, rich in coal and cotton, but almost neglected. Though Manchuria grows rice and tobacco in any quantity, little attention has as yet been paid to it. The harbour of Nicolaievsk being in winter frozen over, and therefore useless at that period of the year, the Chinese have sold to Russia this remote but very desirable slice of Asia, including the coast from the mouth of the Amur as far south as Victoria Bay, where the country of the Koreans begins.

This tract of newly-acquired Russian territory is bounded by the river Usuri, a tributary of the Amur, and is about one hundred and fifty miles in width. But for the purchase of this territory by Russia, the few Manchu Tartars would still have hunted the deer in the grassy solitudes, and the poor Chinese fishermen would still have gathered the sea-weed on the desolate shores.

Being unacquainted with the fact that this purchase had been recently made, we were about to commence the survey of this extensive coast-line, when we became aware of it, while at Olga Bay. So we did not "measure the land," as the Tartars say. We found very few traces of Russian influence and, indeed, although we examined the entire length of coast from Victoria Harbour in the south, to Vladimir Bay in the north, we scarcely ever met a human being, this portion of the vast region of Manchuria being very scantily populated. This immense territory, extending beyond China towards the north and east, has a climate equal to any in Europe, though in winter the cold is very severe, the temperature sometimes falling as low as ten degrees below zero. Our exploration was limited entirely to the coast, which is flat and level, but inland the country is described as very mountainous, the peaks of the Shan-Alin range being twelve thousand feet high and covered with snow which never thaws, even in the summer.

The bear and the deer are in undisputed possession of the forest lands, and herds of half-wild cattle range undisturbed these vast solitudes. We examined the rich pasture lands and wild savannas of the coast-line; but of the inland regions our information was very scanty, as we had no opportunity of penetrating into the interior of the country. The villages, however, are said to be large and populous, and the land is rich and highly cultivated. The population of Manchuria is estimated at fifteen millions.

Renowned for personal bravery above all the peoples of the Mongolian race, this obscure region nourished those conquering Tartars who changed the ruling dynasty of China; and to the present day the original warlike instinct still attaches to the Manchu Tartars, manifesting itself, I believe, as strongly as ever. Military appointments are usually held in China by Tartars, while the more intellectual Chinese fill the higher offices of the State. In the late war with China, the Manchu cavalry charged again and again the British squadrons, but their undoubted valour was of no avail, as they were borne downwards and ridden over by the superior weight of our horses, while the poor "Braves" endeavoured to keep possession of the forts. But what could crossbows avail against Armstrong guns?

Another portion of Manchuria visited by us besides the extensive coast-line alluded to, was that situated at the head of the Gulf of Liao-tung, a territory which is characterised by its level and unvaried appearance. The Gulf of Liao-tung had been very imperfectly surveyed, and we had several perilous adventures and hair-breadth escapes during our explorations of its shallow and treacherous waters. One long night the good ship bumped upon the Bittern shallows; and on another occasion, as we were sailing cautiously along, we spoke a ship steering direct for a dangerous reef, on which in a little time she would have struck, and, in all probability have gone to pieces. On boarding her we found that she was one of the transports engaged during the late war with China in carrying troops and stores, but wofully out of her reckoning, the officers imagining, till they met with us, that she was crossing the China Sea!

Having surveyed the greater portion of the Gulf, we arrived at the mouth of the Liao-tung, where there is a town of some considerable importance, situated at the entrance of the river. On going ashore we found ourselves immediately in the land of pigs, and encompassed by the mud and dirt congenial to these animals. The poor porkers are killed and cured here for the markets of China, and everywhere we were surrounded by numerous bands of victims destined for slaughter. Vicious, long-headed, and obstinate, incredible numbers of them were being driven through the muddy streets, making the place resound with their sharp and piercing cries. Men in huge leathern boots were staggering under sides of bacon; large, flat carts were heaped with brown flitches; boys were reeling under the weight of enormous hams; and boars' heads seemed to gaze reproachfully at you on shop-boards and out of windows. In short, the whole town was filled with evidences of the thriving trade by which the inhabitants gained their living.

Hearing, as we rambled on, a continuous noise in our vicinity, we entered some large, draughty, barn-like buildings, where huge ponderous stones, set upright, were kept revolving round and round by means of oxen, like horses in a mill. On inquiring as to the nature of the operation in which they were engaged, we were told that this was the process of expressing oil from the seeds of the cotton plant, which are afterwards formed into oil-cakes for fattening cattle.

The number of furriers' shops, filled with rich and costly furs, is a striking feature in this outlandish town. The valuable skins of unborn Asiatic lambs

FOOD-PLANTS OF MANCHURIA. 173

from Thibet, sable and martin skins from Eastern Siberia, and tiger skins obtained from the hunters of Mongolia, are here collected in prodigious quantities.

In the flourishing fertile inland plains of Manchuria rice grows in abundance, but in the province of Liao-tung the land is poor and the country not so well supplied with the means of irrigation. In consequence of the more imperfect cultivation of the land only the coarser kinds of cereals and the common food-plants are produced. Besides barley, a kind of millet is cultivated which often grows to an enormous size, and the seeds of which are ground into a sort of meal which, when boiled, forms excellent porridge. Liao-tung is famous for its tobacco, and large quantities of it are planted in the fields higher up the river.

The greater part of Manchuria now belongs to the Chinese; and, as the Russians tried by the destruction of the Polish language to obliterate every sign of Poland, so have the Chinese substituted their own language for that of the Manchu, the Chinese written characters being in daily use. The

Chinese race has so far suppressed the nationality of their former conquerors that even in his own capital, Monkden, the Manchu is hardly his own master. And yet the Manchu seems to have indelibly impressed his mark on the Chinese, for the long, plaited tail now so universally a characteristic of a Chinaman, was originally imposed upon them by the Manchus.

We proceeded next to Dagelet Island where we arrived on the 28th June, at which period the weather was in every way favourable for its examination. It is one of the discoveries of La Perouse, and named after the astronomer of the Astrolabe. As we pulled towards the island I found the description of the renowned navigator very exact. "Very steep," as he says, "but covered with fine trees from the sea-shore to the summit. A rampart of bare rock nearly as perpendicular as a wall completely surrounds it, except seven little sandy coves at which it is possible to land."

We saw the grand central peak towering four thousand feet above us, partially enveloped in clouds. Around its base were huge, detached rocks, some of them four or five hundred feet high, one resembling a sugar-loaf, and another a rude arch. Within a little distance from the shore, numbers of sea-bears, of a reddish-brown colour, came up repeatedly and barked around the boat. The mad pranks and uproarious conduct of these strange ursine creatures offered a striking contrast to the placid demeanour of the gentle Phocæ, or common seals, which only raised their round heads above the water, wonderingly gazed around, and quietly sank again below the surface. Shoals of black-fish rose up further off, baring their dark rounded backs; while several right-whales were spouting in the far distance. Some flying-fish leapt from the water, pursued by a large fish of the mackerel tribe, a noticeable fact,—for seals and flying-fish are not usually seen together. As we neared the island the wave-beaten limestone barrier, weather-stained and variegated with encrusting lichens, towered up from the surface of the sea, crowned with fir-trees, sycamores, and junipers.

The officers of the "Boussole" in La Perouse's voyage did not land, and we were probably the first Europeans who had ever set foot on the island.

The shore is composed of great limestone boulders, worn round by the action of the waves; the tidal rocks are covered with barnacles and limpets; and I observed that Monodonta neritoides, had taken the place of M. labeo, which is the common species on the mainland. The barnacles are Pollicipes and Conia, and the Littorina or periwinkle is similar to that of the mainland.

As we landed in a little bay we perceived three poor Koreans at work. We observed that they were engaged with adze and saw in repairing a dilapidated boat exactly as La Perouse found those he saw eighty years ago. They had dried vast numbers of haliotis or sea-ears, which they string upon rattans for the Chinese market, and sell at the rate of three hundred for a dollar. They likewise collect great heaps of dried seals' flesh, near which I found a dermaster, a silpha, a nitidula, and a staphylinus,—all carrion-beetles.

INTERIOR OF THE ISLAND.

We made our way into the densely-wooded interior by means of the dried-up watercourses, which form steep, rough paths among the trees. Fringing the shore were gigantic Archangelicæ, on the milk-white umbels of which flies, beetles, and bees were numerous. A species of Cissus was trailing over the great round boulders, and here and there was a vine loaded with bunches of small sour grapes. The common thyme and Scrophularia, a little yellow Sedum, and a large blue aster, enlivened the edges of the rocks. The wood was composed of sycamores and junipers, with the Sambucus japonicus, the berries of which are red and not black, as in the common elder. I was curious about the denizens of so small and isolated an island. The birds I observed were cormorants, hawks, gulls, pigeons, blackbirds, sparrows, and small birds like willow-wrens. The Korean fishermen dry large quantities of petrels, leaving their skins in mouldering heaps along the shore. The only indication of a mammal I met with was the skull of a cat, which may have belonged either to a wild species from the mountainous interior of the island, or to a domestic animal wrecked in a junk. I found among molluscs the very peculiar slug of the mainland, a creature with the mantle covering the whole of its back; a little shining land-shell, named Zua, and two species of snails. The only reptile I noticed was a small snake coiled up under a stone. Under the dead fallen leaves and flat stones, I found a centipede about four inches in length; besides two kinds of " thousand-legs," and a large, brown wood-louse, called Armadillidium by naturalists. As for the beetles, they were too numerous to mention. We enjoyed a refection in a small secluded cove, and then pulled partly round the island, admiring many rocky pinnacles and off-lying rugged arches, and then rejoined the ship, which was standing off and waiting for the boat.

There is a charming little bay on the Manchurian coast, which rejoices in the name of Sio-wu-hu. You land on the sandy beach, to the left of a clear running stream, and you see before you a green level plain bounded by distant hills. Cattle and horses graze here, for although the soil is sandy, yet the pasturage is good. The bird's-foot trefoil grows on it, in company with many grasses not to be distinguished from those of England,—the very dandelion seems the same. On the outlying precincts and among the young oaks which skirt the plain, that glorious wide-mouthed blue-bell, Platycodon grandiflora, blooms in all its pride, and Trollius asiaticus is as common as buttercups in a Hampshire meadow. Now the Manchurian bulls have stamped bare patches in this small savannah, and have also left *other* traces of their presence. In these deposits, associated with Aphodius, Geotrupes, and Onthophagus, all shard-beetles, we discover "Sisyphus!" You suppose we easily win this prize. On the contrary, its acquisition was made with considerable difficulty.

What is that dark body moving steadily and slowly across the plain? It is a herd of cattle commanded by a patriarch bull, with a great black head, reddish eyes, short horns, and a dewlap that nearly touches the ground. We are serenely engaged in disentombing Sisyphus, and just looking up we continue our occupation. The moving mass of cows and calves, led on by the patriarch, steadily advances. There are many stoppages, much pawing of the ground, and some low bellowings, but—onward it comes. Prudence suggests a retreat; courage, and a desire for more specimens of Sisyphus, urge our remaining. So, putting on an indifferent air, we go on turning over the sandy deposits. This seems to have some effect on the bovine party. The patriarch bull, his admiring cows and offspring, the playful calves, make a dead halt and stand staring. Thus we continue while a shard remains unexamined, when we rise and, resuming our stick, stroll, with a would-be-careless air, towards the beach. The patriarch bull with the great curly head and dewlap, and all his wives and concubines, follow us down to the water, where, luckily a boat being handy, we leave them. Whether our small stercoraceous ebon friend, with the gray, curved hind legs, of these Tartarean regions, be the Sisyphus Schæfferi of the illustrious Swede, or a new species not yet described, remains for the present a mystery.

* * * * *

The Manchu Tartars are strongly made and active, as befits the life they lead, for are they not all hunters and well acquainted with the chase? Their rifle and their wolf-like dogs are their constant companions. The men chiefly differ from their Chinese associates in their lank black hair being parted in the middle, and hanging down behind in two long plaited tails. Their dress is similar to that of the Chinese, and they are never without a knife and a tobacco-pouch adorned with blue beads. Snakes being troublesome in the long grass they bind straw round their legs like Irish reapers.

The Manchu women we met were clothed in loose blue jackets, close round the neck, and reaching as far as the waist, and fastened with loops on the right side; a petticoat of a bright red reaching half way below the knee. Their legs were bound round with straw as a defence against snake-bites, and covered with spiral strips of red, white, and blue cloth. On the wrists they wore brass and white metal bracelets; their hair was worn in two long tails, reaching to the waist, with narrow strips of red cloth at the ends. There was an ornament at the back of the head between the tails, a leathern band edged with blue beads, with a central line of cowries and brass beads hanging below it. Their earrings were of silver, with pendent brass rings and jade-stone ornaments; and a small ring of silver, with a glass drop to it, was worn through the right ala of the nose. An old lady of the party, having a partiality for spirits, helped herself to friend Buckley's collecting bottle, containing rum—and beetles. The latter she imagined to be there to add a piquancy to the former, but could not make up her mind to swallow them.

The deer, which are numerous on the plains, are hunted at early dawn, as they come to drink in the small streams, among the long grass, at the bottom of the broad valleys. The hunters creep on their hands and knees, and on the slightest alarm throw themselves down, and then again cautiously advance till within certain range, when they fire, and usually bring down their quarry.

I had pictured the land of the Manchus as bleak and barren, but I found myself, as it were, in a great garden run wild. From the sandy banks of a small trout stream, where plenty of fish were rising, I was surrounded by large crimson roses, white-flowered peonies, spotted tiger-lilies, a scarlet single-flowered lychnis, clusters of clematis with dark, hairy, bell-shaped blossoms, lilies of the valley, tall blue-flowered Polymoniums, and the bright yellow blossoms of Trollius asiaticus. The rest of the vegetation was made up of oak-scrub, plume-like sedges, tall grasses, and the stems of a giant Archangelica, with here and there Geranium pratense and a pretty red Valerian.

Beetles turned up in great abundance, the dear cuckoo was heard repeating over and over its favourite monotone, and the skylark overhead was singing gloriously.

Besides some fine examples of Acusta læta, a delicate snail, we observed members of a fine Succinea, or amber-snail, on the broad-ribbed leaves of a species of Hotcia, which grows abundantly in the moist places. The incessant attacks of mosquitoes and sand-flies, however, obliged us frantically to fly from this locality to drier and more elevated ground.

CHAPTER XIV.

Wild Cattle—The Dog and his Master—A Haul of Salmon—Seaweed-collecting Fishermen—A Jovial Crew—A Weakness for Skulls—Olga Bay—Capture of a strange Insect—Place of Refuge for Old Seals—Appearance of three Ainos—St. Vladimir Bay—A Useful Beacon—The Emerald Wing.

BEEF was wanted by our sailors, and the owner of some half-wild cattle was willing to sell, provided the animals could be caught. The beasts, which at this leafy period are out in the wilderness, revelling in the luxuriant grasses, are very difficult to approach. A party of seamen, however, eager for the fun, were furnished with ropes and running bowlines; and after much tearing through brushwood, floundering in swamps, shouting, laughing, and mad excitement, succeeded in making prisoners of two little plump, bright-eyed bullocks. I followed in the wake of this merry party, and in my scramble I never saw a country so entirely given up to nature. Hardly any traces of man were visible—the only signs I saw were straggling herds, and an occasional deer's head, gnawed by the dogs of the Manchu hunters.

On one occasion, as we were hauling the seine, a noble Tartar deer-hound, fawn-coloured, and with a splendid brush for a tail, picked a quarrel with another dog of less degree, the bone of contention, so to speak, being a fish's head. In the fight which followed, the Tartar was the conqueror, and so excited the admiration of the First Lieutenant that he set his affections upon him; but the master of Quilee—for so the dog was named—a poor Chinese fisherman, was loth to part with his "friend on all fours." Actually, though a Chinaman, he was insensible to the temptation of dollars! The First Lieutenant was greatly disappointed because he could not prevail upon the poor fisherman to part with the animal; but suddenly a brilliant idea flashed across his mind—recklessly stripping off his coat, he offered it for Quilee. The brass buttons and gold lace were too much for the Mongol.

Poetically speaking, he should have seized the faithful hound in his arms, and rushed wildly away, after the manner of the Bedouin and his beautiful Arab mare!

In the evening the seine was hauled with much success. We landed at the first cast twenty-three very fine salmon, their weight ranging from three-and-a-half to fourteen pounds; and a few small turbot from three to six pounds each. We caught next a shark six feet long. In all we took thirty-nine salmon, most of them from eight to fourteen pounds; half-a-dozen turbot; and a bucket-full of fine prawns. The salmon were the Salmo orientalis of Pallas, and the pretty spotted species named S. leucomaensis. The "turbot" of the sailors, I believe, is the Japanese halibut (Hippoglossus olivaceus). The hideous star-gazer, with its great staring eyes, starting from the top of its rough, spiny head, the Japanese bass, and Burgher's gurnard, were likewise taken. All these fish, enough to allow the ship's company a pound and a-half per man, were taken amongst the tangled masses of Laminaria and the narrow grass-like Zostera, in the brackish water near the mouth of a little river which runs into Sio-wu-hu Bay.

Near the shore were several temporary conical huts, owned by a lot of migratory seaweed-collecting fishermen. They spread the broad glutinous fronds of the Laminaria in the sun, and after they are thoroughly dried, collect them in large bundles, which they stack, covering them with coarse matting and straw. These miserably poor men are wonderfully expert in the management of their narrow canoes, which they form from the trunk of a single tree. They spear the salmon, upon which they chiefly feed, by torchlight, using as torches large pieces of birch bark. Although so poor they seem contented with their lot, and, in the evening, after the labours of the day, smoke and chat, and make discordant music by playing on certain quaint reed-pipes.

I landed again with the seining party, for, besides the exciting pleasure of catching good fish, there was a chance of securing something interesting to the naturalist, if not good for the "pot." We chose a shallow sandy bay, full of "tangle," where a little rivulet runs into the sea, for in such localities do the salmon love to congregate. It was evening, and the poor Chinese fishermen had hauled their canoes high up on the beach. They had lighted their wood fires, and were peaceably employed, some smoking, and others preparing the supper of fish. Huge rocks, crowned with trees, dark and solemn in the twilight, formed the background ; and already the fire-flies had commenced their intermittent illumination. The seine was taken out in the "jolly-boat," and formed a vast semicircle in the water. The sailors were scattered through the bush, cutting down trees, and making huge fires to attract the fish. Soon parties in long boots or with bare legs assembled at either end of the seine, and singing songs, if not select, yet cheery, commenced hauling in the net. Glittering scales and silvery bellies soon showed themselves above the water ; and as the seine was landed amid great excitement, a tumbling, leaping mass of fish was thrown upon the sand.

"Here's a kinger," cries one of the sailors, as he "fists" a noble salmon.

"Only a toader," cries another, casting high up among the bushes an ugly brown Tetraodon.

"Here's an *adjective* big turbot," says a short man, with a rubicund proboscis.

"Here's shrimp sauce for the turbot," says a long, pale boy, with a squint in his eye, picking up prawns three inches long.

"Here," sings out another of the jovial crew, "is a curio for the Doctor."

With that, a hairy man of the sea brought me a large, yellow, somewhat apathetic crab, with the query, "Please, sir, is this any good; I never seed another like 'im?" I thanked him courteously, and took possession of a splendid, perfect, living specimen of Telmessus serratus, a rare crab of goodly size.

* * * * *

The remark of the "needy knifegrinder" to the compassionate gentleman who inquired into his history, "Story! God bless you, I have none to tell, sir," will equally apply to me. And yet, as I meditate over a quiet pipe in my floating sanctum, each bone and skull that hangs around me recalls certain little incidents which I am unwilling to keep entirely to myself. That little cramped foot reminds me of the bombardment of Canton, and was taken from an unfortunate woman who was killed by one of our shells. That baby-skeleton points to the prevalence of infanticide in China, for its owner was drowned in the Pearl River by its unnatural parent. That mummified fœtal deer brings before my mind's eye the shaven-pated doctors of Japan, who find in such as that a valuable remedy.

I confess to a weakness for skulls: from the simple cartilaginous rudiment of the cuttle-fish to the ample dome where intellect once sat supreme, they have all great attractions in my eyes. When, therefore, I "pitch my foot" against a skull, like Hamlet, Prince of Denmark, I take it up, and regard it with speculative interest. I touch lightly, however, on the bleached human skulls I obtained by the banks of the Pearl River. Suffice it to say that several, in beautiful preservation, adorn my collection. In one I discovered in a "chatty" on the green summit of Tiger Island, a snake had formed her nest; and another in my possession was the plaything of little Chinese children, who were rolling it about on the ground.

For many skulls I am indebted to the prowess of our sportsmen. My seals are from Todomosiri, my great eagle is from Manchuria, my Moschus crania are from the Korea, and my albatross and giant petrel from the broad bosom of the Atlantic. Others are of my own procuring. Thus, my turtles and my pigmy deer were from Sunda Strait; my scaly ant-eater is from Whampoa; my Babirusa's skull is a present; and a few were purchased from Canton old curiosity shops. My largest skull once belonged to an antlered monarch of Manchuria, and its acquisition was made in the following way. A party had leapt on shore at Sio-wu-hu, and, like young horses just let loose, had dispersed themselves in various directions for a glorious run. Some scoured the plain, rejoicing in their liberty, and gathered great bunches of roses and peonies; some wandered thoughtfully along the strand, thinking possibly of home and Polly; one, gun in hand, dived among the oak-woods, intent on game; and one, sweeping-net aloft, waded gleefully among the flowers. Just as the sun was declining, and all were thinking of going on board, a form approached from across the plain, like amorous Falstaff at Herne's old oak, huge antlers branching out above his head, a vasculum, cram-full of plants, across his back, and in each hand blushing floral trophies. It was Wilford of the "seven-league boots," who had found the cervine relic in the woods.

One day I was sauntering along a path, winding, narrow, and irregular, by the side of a rocky gully in Tsu-Sima, an island in the Korea Strait. The scene around me was very beautiful. The gurgling water rolled clear and sparkling over its stony bed, except where a big boulder checked its even course, when a deep pool was formed, where little trout-like fish calmly disported themselves. The sides of the ravine, clothed with leafy beauty, rose up around; and trees of great variety, waving their green heads in the soft sea-breeze, were springing from every rift in the slate-stone rocks. Onward I strolled, now taking a snail from the bushes, and anon making prisoner of a longicorn, till I emerged, from under the wild mulberry-trees, upon an upland slope, green and pleasant to the eye, and bordered with dark woods and yellow raspberry-bushes. Suddenly my attention is arrested. What is that white gleaming object in the grass? A cranium of some unknown deer of Japan? Nay, smile not, gentle reader; 'tis a horse's skull!

We were now in Olga Bay, a deep inlet, ending in a river, with wild, uncultivated, rocky sides, covered with wood from the water's edge. I worked my way from near the entrance to where a party was hauling the seine on the right bank, wading through long, rank grass, sweeping for insects among the flowers, and beating the young oaks, all the while stumbling over mouldering trunks of trees, and loose, old, moss-grown stones. Thus

I wandered on in the clear sunshine, along the sandy shore, with its heaps of drift wood; picking up ground-beetles under great chips of trees, felled long ago by hunters; detecting Cecina manchurica, a new form of mollusk, under damp logs near the sea. I was half maddened by mosquitoes in the cool shade of crowded trees; the gauze veil which I shipped in despair to guard my face from their attacks half blinded me.

A strange insect in the air, flying like a longicorn, arrested my attention. At risk of broken shins I gave chase to it, and captured it. I found it to be a Myrmeleon-like Neuropteron, with curious cup-shaped knobs at the end of its long antennæ. I passed on among the prostrate branches of a huge linden tree, lately felled by fishermen, and still laden with blossoms, from which bees were busy extracting nectar. I came across bushes crowded with Canthari, or blistering-beetles, of a pale red colour, with green head and thorax. Hearing an ominous rustle of dead leaves on the dry, elevated ground, I looked and saw the slow, fat, undulating form of a great-headed adder, angrily making his way from the invader of his solitude.

While pursuing my researches, I suddenly came upon a stone arch of uneven granite, rude, natural, and Cyclopean, overgrown with weeds, mottled with lichens, and half-concealed by a rank undergrowth, yet a veritable arch of rugged stone. It suggested the idea of those rough-hewn stones of Stonehenge, and the primæval altars, built by white-robed, bearded Druids, on plains and in sacred groves full of mistletoe-covered oaks, for purposes of mystic and most probably unholy worship. Under this rude arch I crept with a childish kind of pleasure, although to have gone round it would have been far easier. .The strong lines of a spider's web of unusual size, with a fat, bloated occupant in the centre, opposed my progress, but only for a moment; Arachne's web was rent, and the "long-legged spinner" placed in durance vile. When at length fatigued with my exertions, I was reposing on a log near the shore, I observed not very far off a something in the drift, which, on examination, turned out to be an imperfect skull of Steno, a genus of true dolphins.

To the north of Cape Notoro, in Aniwa Bay, Saghalien, is a rocky and lonely spot. It is a long, low point, projecting into the beautiful wide bay, composed of great rounded rocks and drifted shingle. Here, sheltered by the granite boulders, and concealed by coarse grass and reeds, come the old and the sick of the seal tribe which inhabit these waters, to seek refuge from their fellows, and to breathe their last in peace. The impress of their huge bodies may be traced on the dead, soiled, flattened herbage.

From the quantity of bones strewn about the place, I think this must be the chief cemetery of these poor animals. The only sounds that disturb the silence are the harsh notes of wild swans passing high overhead, and the frightened caw of a rook, soaring, dodging, and trying in vain to elude the pursuit of a determined hawk. The solitary wildness of the spot is hardly relieved by the unexpected appearance of three Ainos, aborigines of

Saghalien, who have come over the neighbouring cliffs to gaze upon the brown-haired strangers. These stand motionless and silent, watching our every movement with a fixed and wondering stare. Long, white, spinous processes of the dorsal vertebræ of a whale, sticking up above the grass, look like tombstones of departed Phocæ. I discovered here a rare prize, in the skull of a large seal, with a vertical bony crest extending from the frontal bone to the occiput. An imperfect skull of the Halicore, or dugong, was another grand addition to the number of my specimens. I obtained, besides, the crania—both, alas! much injured—of two species of Delphinus, or true dolphins.

We were now in St. Vladimir Bay, a wide and deep recess on the Manchurian coast, a little north of Olga. Sea-cliffs bound the long, curved outline of the bay, their summits green with oaks. Below them the ground is level, and a belt of verdure extends from the cliffs to the water's edge. The undergrowth is dark and humid, and the number of fallen trees, in various states of decay, promise well for snails, slugs, and fungus-loving beetles. Boleti stud their rotting boles, and in these Mycetophagi reward our diligent research. Shade of Fabricius! what swarms of insect life! The ants alone are worthy the pen of Nylander; and as for the spiders, the erudition of Walckenaer, and the industry of Blackwall, would be needful to portray their varied forms, and illustrate their wondrous instincts. I penetrated a thicket, where bushes, laden with bunches of currants, grew all around. While feeding on these with the greedy voracity of a schoolboy, my attention was diverted to a split bamboo, with the valve of a Pecten, or scallop-shell, stuck in the fissure. A nearer scrutiny assured me this was meant as an indication of *water;* and lo! a clear pool lay hid among the herbage. Some wandering Tartar had been here, and, having slaked his thirst, had in gratitude placed this useful beacon. But what is that suspended from a bough which overhangs the beach? It is a skull, the skull of a bear, for the lower jaw and other bones of the defunct

Bruin are lying on the shingle beneath; and there hangs his cranium, so far beyond my reach that I was disposed to leave with some exclamation like that of the fox when disappointed of the grapes. Some of the sailors, however, I thought might be able to obtain it for me. As good-luck would have it, the sailors happened to want water, and came here for it. Close at hand was a tiny spring, from which distilled a slender, trickling rivulet from the cliff, filling an excavation in the shingle, which, being enlarged, a goodly cistern was formed. By means of a hose and Earl's engine, the cold, clear water was speedily transferred into a canvas tank in the pinnace; and in due time one of the sailors undertook to get possession of the cranium for me. Mounting with the agility peculiar to his class, he soon had the prize in his hands, and descending quickly, laid it at my feet.

Between the little river which runs through the plain at the head of the bay and the stony, rank, weed-grown little hills on the right, is a narrow, grassy strip, thickly studded with the green culms and broad white umbels of a gigantic species of Archangelica, and where Solomon's-seal, and Trollius orientalis, grow in the wildest profusion. A long, grey Lixus, or snout-beetle, bores into all the stems of the Archangelica, drilling round holes with his cylindrical snout. Here Buckley found an "emerald wing," the elytron, or wing-cover, of a genus of Buprestidæ, or gold-beater, which was greatly admired by the coleoptero-maniacs. Every man of them is desirous of obtaining the perfect insect. Some go north, and some south. The plains are scoured, the mountains climbed, and the valleys searched; but all their researches are in vain. " 'Tis not in mortals to command success."

I think it rather hard that unsuccessful efforts are usually consigned to oblivion. Successful results are triumphantly set forth. The discovery of new genera—the detection of beautiful forms for the first time brought to light by the insect-net or the dredge—are duly recorded with pride and gratification; but who shall chronicle the failures, the keen disappointments, the labour thrown away, and the energy and enterprise fruitlessly expended in such researches? How disappointing it is, when tons of mud have been sifted, when bushels of sand have been examined, when huge stones have been laboriously upturned, and when the bushes have been beaten in despair, to discover nothing to reward all this labour, nothing to kindle hope or animate to future exertions—not even a beetle to reward the patient enthusiast.

To return, however, to the "emerald wing!" Collinson the indefatigable was seen minutely scrutinising the fissured bark of old trunks, and the sound bark of stately trees, peering, like a jackdaw, into rotten wood, or scratching up the earth like a terrier who suspects he is on the trail of a rat. On a sudden, riveting his gaze on a young oak, he gave utterance to a cry as wild and exulting as an Indian war-whoop; for he had seen the owner of the "emerald wing" sunning itself on the tender green surface of a leaf. This reminded me of another great hunt for an emerald beetle (Drypta emarginata) with old Turner, a poor but far-famed and eccentric

Collector of Insects, now no more, in Hampshire, at pretty Alverstoke. In vain we toiled and tore up the grassy bank, the old man growling and swearing in a deep undertone at Anchomenus prasinus, another green but common bettle, which was always running out and giving him false hopes. At length he found a veritable Drypta. Drawing a long breath, he exclaimed, this time aloud, and with a jubilant expression, "Glory! glory! glory! I got 'un!"

CHAPTER XV.

Expedition to a Lake—Search for New Specimens—Change of Scene—Manchurian Flowers—Crickets and Grasshoppers—Dragon-flies—Trapa natans—"Dash" discomfited—A Picnic Party—Capture of Crustaceans—Enthusiastic Beetle-hunters—Skeleton Trees—Cryptochiton Stelleri—An Impressive Scene.

WHILST still at anchor in this pleasant Bay of Vladimir, we heard of a lake not very far distant, and determined to explore it. We were greatly tempted to this expedition by the beauty of the weather, which, indeed, was glorious. The boat was got ready—a light, four-oared gig—and a little dredge was soon placed in the stern-sheets. A modest bottle of beer, and a few other creature comforts, were provided for us; and "away flew the light bark o'er the silvery bay." As we approached the shore, the round head of a seal came up alongside the boat, and his wondering eyes gazed seriously at the "merry men" bending to their oars.

AN OFFERING TO THE DOCTOR. 205

Our sporting messmate essayed to shoot a cormorant, which was sitting, gorged with fish, on the low, dark rocks that showed their dangerous backs above the water, but was unsuccessful. The handsome, black-tailed gulls, unused to firearms, were not disturbed by the report, but continued to hover boldly around; and the little guillemots, in pairs, dived about, or flew in a straight line over the surface of the bay. But what has that little party of sailors, struggling under the weight of some unwonted curio, picked up along the shore? As we land, they bear it aloft with an air of triumph, and with comic gravity lay it as an offering at the doctor's feet. It is the dorsal vertebra of a whale!

On landing, we had again to launch our boat in a stream which would conduct us to the waters of the lake; but before we could do so, we had to haul it over a bed of loose shingle, and this demanded the tug of war. All hands assisted, and after great exertions, accompanied with some rather strong language, we succeeded; but the amount of pushing, dragging, shouting, wading, struggling, and splashing, before we managed to get our slender gig again afloat, was almost incredible. When again seated in the boat, we shortly after found ourselves in the channel which nearly connects the lake with the waters of the bay.

Notwithstanding all this excitement, and the novelty of the scene, I did not forget to look after new specimens. Near the salt-water shore I observed a large blue Salvia mingling with the red flowers of Sedum Telephium and the yellow hawkweed; but as we approached the fresh-water shore, these plants were replaced by a gay yellow Iris and a blue Lobelia. Alarmed at our approach a quail rose with a sudden whirr, and a hawk was disturbed taking his noonday meal on a stone, the feathers of his prey forming a circle all around him. Swifts were hovering in considerable numbers overhead, and as we neared the lake, we saw ducks and gulls disporting themselves on its calm surface.

The first thing we did was to pull to the other

end, sounding as we went with a hand lead. We found the lake very shallow, having only twenty-one feet in the deepest part. The bottom, we observed, was composed of soft black mud, and, towards the shallow further extremity, of fine clean sand; the circumference being bounded by a belt of shingle. The water was perfectly fresh, very clear, and extremely free from weeds. We noticed but few fish, and no trout or salmon. Several plaice and mullet were, however, caught in the narrow channel leading from the lake to the bay. The only crustacean visible was the "hairy-handed crab," Eriocheir japonicus. In the sandy parts the dredge supplied us with numerous fine specimens of a dark-brown, black Corbicula, but this bivalve appeared to be the only molluscous inhabitant of the lake. In the swampy pools of the immediate vicinity, however, we obtained two species of a pond-snail, or Planorbis, but could not detect the presence of either Ancylus or Limnæa.

We left our boat now to explore the woods around. In traversing the swampy plain in the bight of the deep bay, we captured several large black and yellow Lepturas in the overblown peonies. We also swept with our net the rank grass for jumping Halticas and golden Chrysomelas. As we ascended the green hill-side, the grass appeared to grow higher and higher, till at last we became buried in a dense scrub of hazels and young oaks. We were also made painfully aware of those intolerable pests, the mosquitoes. Around us were numerous seared and blackened skeleton trees, rearing their gaunt, weird, leafless forms above the verdure. There were others, however, of nobler proportions, through whose great spreading branches we could spy the lovely pied woodpecker exploring their rugged trunks, and sounding for rotten places with his pick-like beak. With the exception of a chattering magpie, and a little shy ground-squirrel scampering over the fallen trees, we saw no other sign of animal life in the still, dark wood.

On emerging, however, from the umbrage of the trees, into the open spaces near the borders of the lake, the aspect of the scene was entirely changed.

The humming-bird hawkmoth was seen hovering over the thistle-heads. Longicorn beetles could be perceived winging their way, steady and undeviating, as is their wont, over the neighbouring tree-tops. The tall Mecalopses and Hoteias had run to seed, the roses were gone, the great white peonies were mostly withered, and the petals of the scarlet lychnis were no longer bright. In their places, however, we saw the large expanded bells of Platycodon grandiflora in every grassy spot among the young oaks; the monkshood and larkspur, the tiger-lily and the Chinese pink in full bloom. The "great noisy world" of orthopterous insects here seemed to reign supreme. In the tall, flowery grass, among the blooming undergrowth, in the foliage of the young oaks, on the tops of moss-covered stones, and by the reedy margins of the brook, they hopped, chirped, croaked, and hissed. I never saw so many crickets and grasshoppers congregated in one spot, so variegated in colour, so varied in form. There were green and brown, solitary and social; with short legs and long legs;

P

singing and skipping for very wantonness, because the sun was shining so gaily, and the late shower had made the tender grass so green and toothsome. And then the dragon-flies! Gauze-winged beauties with flat yellow bodies, delicately alighting for an instant on some dead twig; chasing each other vehemently across the swampy pools, or dashing wildly before your face in their eager pursuit of prey.

As we approached the shores of the lake, we traversed a marshy spot fragrant with mint, and covered here and there with great patches of tansy and southernwood. Here, also, gleaming amid the rushes, were the pure white flowers of the Grass of Parnassus. Hundreds of little green tree-frogs were squatting flat on the broad leaves of the colts-foot; and anon, a warty toad scrambled through the moist grass, or a graceful harmless snake glided silently towards the water. In the shallow parts of the lake itself we saw green patches of Trapa natans, a water plant, its four-horned curious fruit, and radiating leaves with buoy-like footstalks, forming light and elegant rafts upon the water. Along the weedy margin a few sanderlings and plovers were feeding, and as we looked across, a wild duck suddenly emerged from the rushes, and with great noise, and splashing with his wings, struck across the shallow water.

We cooked our crabs, smoked our pipes, and spent a glorious day. The incidents which befell some of our party were neither numerous nor sensational, yet, perhaps, they deserve some mention. As we were sauntering along, the little dog "Dash," pricking up his ears, disappeared in a very excited state in the bush, but shortly made his appearance discomfited and crest-fallen. His ears and mouth were scratched and bleeding, and we imagined he had done battle with a marten or a badger, and had got the worst of it. B—— also had an unfortunate encounter, though the result in his case was that he was more alarmed than hurt. While patiently fishing in the stream, he was bitten by a snake. . The doctor of course was at once sent for, and his attention was directed to the wound with a look of serious inquiry. After a scientific examination of the reptile's mouth, however, he saw there was no danger, for no poison-fangs were to be seen. He was able, therefore, to appease the patient's anxiety by inspiring him with the confident anticipation of a speedy cure.

In making the tour of the lake, we found our progress on several occasions interrupted by narrow streams from the hills. Some of these we bounded over, and through some of them we waded; but there was one too wide for leaping, and too deep for wading. We were, therefore, under the necessity of stripping, and as we required our clothes on the other side, we tied them in a bundle and lashed them to the tops of our heads. A few strokes then carried us across, with our garments perfectly dry, and in a state to be resumed at once.

* * * * *

We again found here in Manchuria the crab with a hairy hand (Eriocheir japonicus). The manner of our meeting with this curious creature was in this wise. We had joined a pic-nic to the lake. There was Wilford of the "seven-league boots," vasculum on back, intent on plants; there was Buckley, fishing-rod in hand, eager for salmon; Sutherland, thoughtful, caring for beetles; and the doctor, renewing his youth in the fellowship of that gay band. At length, fatigued with our several exertions, for even pleasure sometimes becomes a toil, we lay supine upon the sand, under the shade of the hazels that fringed the margin of the lake. While one was preparing the soothing pipe, another, prone over the water, was taking huge horse-like draughts of the limpid element. As sailors ashore must always light a fire, some collected little sticks for the inside, while others picked up larger boughs for the outside. A spark was speedily produced in a bunch of dried grass, which was waved in the air till a blaze was created, and the fire was then kindled.

A fire, however, without anything to cook is bad, so we cast about for something to eat. We had a fowling-piece, but there were no birds to shoot. The fishes would not allow themselves to be caught, and for beetles we had no appetite. Crabs, however, there were in such abundance that we had only to pick and choose. So we waded, bare-legged, into the lake, and in the shallows of the fresh-water we captured these desirable crustaceans, of the species known as Eriocheir japonicus. Each specimen as it was captured was cast upon the glowing embers. Biscuit we had, and wild onions grew in the sand around. Serene and undisturbed in that wild spot, where no boatswain's pipe assailed our ears, where no "bear a hand" was heard, and where the noise and bustle of the ship were quite forgotten, we thankfully cooked our crabs, and enjoyed our frugal meal.

Some "Innocent" not yet versed in the deep mysteries of beetle-lore, and not inured to the toils of beetle-hunting, who may never have seen, as I have, the indefatigable Doctor Power on his stomach in a ditch, spectacles on nose, and the perspiration streaming down his cheeks with his fossorial exertions, may imagine that because I have some thousand beetles nicely carded in my store-box, I have had no trouble but to pick them up. I can tell that complacent know-nothing that he is quite mistaken. With what exertions, for instance, are those great carnivorous ground-beetles, the Carabi, taken! One would stare with amazement at certain enthusiasts (for I have imbued many with the love of beetles) rushing wildly over the boulders and large flat stones in dried-up watercourses, at the "imminent deadly risk" of bruised shins and sprained ankles, eager in the pursuit of tantalizing, active Cicindelæ, huge stones upturned in their course over the plain, and their habiliments torn as they forced their way through the scrub along some beach-fringing belt of trees. Here in Manchuria we used to land in a ship's boat, and were left to the tender mercies of the mosquitoes and bears; the gnats being put first because their name is legion, and their torment is nearly unbearable. Bears, however, are so "few and far between," that although I have several of their skulls, I only had a good look at one, and he escaped with his valuable life, though several of us thirsted for his blood. We then forced our way breast-high in tangled brushwood, long, hard grass, and creepers and bamboos, up the sloping sides of the sea-skirting hills, and when we reached the top, we found it comparatively level, and instead of being breast-high in brushwood, were agreeably surprised to see it knee-deep in flowers—peonies, monkshood, Hoteias, and Campanulas. In such a scene the trees are large, and animal life in various forms is astir. The pied woodpecker is scrutinising the whereabouts of grubs, and giving now and then an inquiring tap, while the little striped ground-squirrel plays at hide-and-seek among the branches of fallen trees. The head of a startled deer may be seen for an instant—a long brown nose, and two mild inquiring eyes—and then a portion of his other extremity, as he bounds away in the dim vistas of the trees.

One thing that strikes us in this wild green wilderness is the prodigious number of those charred and blackened trees that strew the ground in every direction, though often so overgrown with weeds that one becomes acquainted with them in a way generally more practical than pleasant, namely, by finding himself on his face among the flowers, his shins barked, and his temper ruffled. This phenomenon is owing to the wandering shooting and fishing parties of Manchu Tartars, who always fire the scrub and burn down the trees, to clear the land and make it yield good pasturage. It is under these burnt logs that Carabs "most do congregate;" and the labour required to dislodge and capture them is really no joke. Two small bipeds, energetic and determined, one at each end of an immense blackened log, can, however, soon move it by well directed efforts, assisted by sundry encouraging exclamations, as "There, she moves," "Now then, doctor," or "Again, again, again!" Thus the log is turned over, and my amiable and worthy colleague, Sutherland, or my impetuous messmate, Buckley, share with me possibly one or two fine Carabi; perhaps a neat black species with grooved elytra, perhaps the gorgeous Carabus smaragdinus in all his emerald glory, perhaps one equally as large, green and beautiful, with rows of beads on his wing-covers, or a small, brown, flattish species. Besides these you may bag a few specimens of Helops and Helops' cousins-german, and sometimes a stag-beetle will reward our persevering exertions. But oh! what sweeps we look as we return in triumph with our capture! Our nether habiliments, now no longer white, torn and stained, our hands decidedly "dirty paws," and our faces as smutty as the bottom of the family tea-kettle!

* * * * *

After a severe gale I landed on a warm calm day in the bight of the bay, and the contrast between the clear sunshine and the smiling aspect of the green shore, and the late raging sea and driving spray, was very grateful. The sand-pipers were quietly busy probing for worms in the saturated, spongy soil. One very pretty species, with broad webs to his feet, was hovering about the surf, chasing flies, and even swimming leisurely about in the water. Cormorants were dressing their coarse plumage on the rocks, the black-tailed gulls were sporting over the now tranquil sea, and the inland pond, where the water-fowl used to hide, was twice its original size, so that the rushes no longer concealed the timid widgeon ducks and teal. The little streams were swollen into small torrents; the shingle was tossed up upon the grassy plain; the rushes were swept over and torn up by the roots; the outline of the beach even was altered, and the force of the wind and the violence of the sea were shown by the fact that thousands of large mussels in bunches and clusters had been wrenched from their anchorage on the rocks, and were thrown up high and dry upon the strand.

Crossing a narrow promontory, I descended the cliffs on the other side, and reached the seaward shore. I found myself in a small bay, — high, jagged, limestone pinnacles, and huge vertical-seamed cliffs, hedging me in and bounding the view on either side, while in front was the open treacherous main. The first objects I noticed were prodigious masses of tangle, or Laminaria, thrown up in heaps, and hundreds of the large tunicated curious Cryptochiton Stelleri, a sort of coat-of-mail mollusk, detached by the gale from the off-lying submerged rocks, and cast, like shipwrecked sailors, on the shore. Dashed against the cliffs and ground by rolling boulders, their internal valves were mostly crushed, and here and there their mangled bodies were found, having been carried to the tops of rounded stones, and their bones picked clean by sea birds. I walked solitary and musing, up and down the bay, throwing mutilated Chitons by dozens into the sea, and was rewarded now and then by finding one tolerably perfect. Several specimens of the large Octopus, or cuttlefish—possibly the rather apocryphal O. chinensis—had been cast ashore, and I had thus an opportunity of securing the horny mandibles, the rudimentary skull, and some of the suckers from the arms. One I measured was six feet from the tip of one arm to the tip of the opposite arm. The large eyes of this creature are covered with the skin, with the exception of a small round aperture; the body is black, brown, and minutely granular. Large skate, rock cod, and other fish which had shared the untimely fate of the cuttles, were lying dead and bruised among the stones, and fragments of the giant Lithodes, or stone-crab, (like the monster I sent to the British Museum) strewed the narrow strips of sand. It was an impressive scene, and remains indelibly stamped upon my memory.

CHAPTER XVI.

Risiri—Effects of a Violent Gale—Rifunsiri Island—Deserted Fishing Sheds—Todomosiri or Seal Island—Aniwa Bay—The Duck Family in Full Feather—Ornithology of the Island—Abodes of the Ainos—A Domestic Scene—Dress of the Men—Feminine Ornament—The Hairy Kuriles.

On the 15th September, 1859, we arrived at Risiri, situated on the south side of the western entrance to La Pérouse Strait. This little island was mistaken by La Pérouse for a mountain on the mainland of Yesso, and was named by him "Pic de Langle." The entire island, with the exception of a narrow strip of scoria land which fringes the coast, is composed of a great conical volcanic peak, which rises bold and rugged to the height of 6000 feet above the level of the sea. Its summit is white with snow, and in clear weather is visible at a distance of 70 or 80 miles. It is about thirty miles in circumference.

Near the spot where we landed, the side of the

cone has been split open, and a wild headlong torrent is now rushing with a mighty roar down the side. It was only a few days after the great gale, and in this gigantic fissure there were still some fearful evidences of the fury of the storm. Huge trees were torn from their foundations in the rock, and tossed across the roaring torrent, the bed of which was choked up with great irregular masses of rock which had fallen from above.

In the calm sunshine, viewing this mighty chasm, with the raging torrent, the torn-up trees, and the stupendous rugged cliffs towering around, you are led in imagination to picture to yourself the scene of an earlier age, when, in some fearful convulsion of nature, the vast mountain cone was itself thrown up, vomiting forth flame and smoke.

Rifunsiri Island is situated to the north of Risiri, from which it is separated by a strait about five miles wide. It is eleven miles in a north and south direction, by two and a half wide. It is very rugged, and rises about six hundred feet above the level of the sea.

It is noticed by La Pérouse under the name of Cape Guibert, on the mainland of Yesso. On the east side the island is sloping and fertile, but on the west side it is bold and faced with reefs and sunken rocks.

Here we found very extensive but now deserted fishing sheds for the curing of salmon. Ainos and Japanese were living in neat little houses, with patches of cultivated vegetables growing all around them.

There is no place where one can have better opportunities of seeing seals in the privacy of domestic life, living unmolested in their island home, than Todomosiri, in the Gulf of Tartary. As, however, that little spot is a very long way off, and very few are able to visit it, I will endeavour to give some idea of the wild scenes in those out-of-the-way places where whalers put in for water, and take the opportunity of knocking on the head a few hundred seals to complete their cargo.

The small barren island called Monneron by La Pérouse, and Todomosiri, or Seal Island, by the

Japanese, is situated on the north side of the west entrance to La Pérouse Strait. It is a huge mass of bare trachyte, a steep weather-stained rock rising 1500 feet abruptly from the sea, and with some detached rocks on its eastern side. As we approached it, we saw a species of great brown gull, greedy for fish bones and offal, hovering round the base; a lonely cormorant, with outstretched neck, drying her expanded wings on the salient angle of a black crag; and a little hawk soaring high above the summit. These are the only birds that frequent the island; oysters, mussels, and limpets are the only mollusks on its shore; and a carrion-beetle, a large black Silpha, is the only insect met with. There are, however, numerous seals. Many of these were swimming and diving around the island, their uncouth reddish brown heads showing now and then above the surface of the water. Others were basking in the sun, motionless on the broad smooth rocks, the remnants of their fish dinners strewn about them. The bones of some which had died from old age or wounds were bleaching in the wind, and the carcases of others were seen decomposed and torn by gulls and cormorants. The dirt, stench, and strange company, with the wild great rocks towering all around, produced an impression certainly novel, but not altogether agreeable.

We anchored pretty close under the lee of the island, directly opposite a little white shingly cove, with patches of long coarse reedy grass in the background. This is a favourite resort of the seals, and nowhere can their manners and customs be more favourably studied. The old gray bulls rear the fore part of their bodies and slowly sway themselves from side to side, meanwhile throwing up their great heads and bellowing continuously. The cows and their calves are congregated together in a coterie by themselves, and reposing on the outlying rocks, in attitudes anything but graceful, is an entire seraglio of young females. The noise made by the seals during the night is something fearful. One might imagine it to be something like the croaking of Brobdingnag bull-frogs, varied at intervals by deep growls and sharp cries, loud snortings, dissonant brayings, and other sounds of a more unearthly kind. Three individuals fell victims to the prowess of our sportsmen, and were towed on board in triumph.

Aniwa Bay, in the south-east end of the island of Saghaleen, is included between Cape Notoro and Cape Siritoko. It is a very fine bay, forty miles deep. Midway between the two capes there is a depth of fifty-eight fathoms, the water gradually becoming more shallow towards the shore.

On the 27th September we weighed anchor, and were drifted, from daylight to sunset, across the broad bay. There was no wind, and a dense fog covered the surface of the water; but a south-west current took us through the calm, in from eighteen to twenty fathoms, to the north of Cape Notoro. During the day we got one or two casts of the dredge.

Some of the most successful and at the same time agreeable dredging I ever had, was furnished me in this nearly unknown bay. I had a fine boat and a good serviceable dredge, and every haul yielded good results. Many treasures of the sea were brought to light. The crabs were always great favourites of mine, although they are usually more picturesque than beautiful. In their rugged shells and hirsute coats they are frequently grotesque, bizarre, and even absurd in their personal appearance, the shuffling, staring, stalk-eyed, uncouth beings! Some of them have legs upon their backs, by means of which they retain shields formed of sponges, under which they hide themselves. And then their singular habits! They sidle awkwardly along; they feign death; they spitefully snap their claws at you; they defiantly advance; they timidly retreat; they hide themselves in old shells; they wriggle themselves into cracks and crannies of stones, and the labyrinthine recesses of the corals.

And then we have the sponges alcynoid and silicious, which often crowd the dredge and cause an embarrassment of riches, but as their spicula are sharp and irritate the hands, they are usually thrown overboard. Some of them, though wanting in beauty of form, are, however, very lovely in colour.

The coral-makers are often numerous, and even sometimes in warm latitudes too abundant, more especially the smaller Caryophylliæ and their allies.

The lover of the gentle art feels a thrill of joy when a fine trout takes his fly, or a noble salmon is fast to his line; the sportsman is jubilant when he brings down his snipe right and left; the hunter evinces a stern delight when, pierced by his unerring ball, the king of beasts lies dead at his feet. So likewise does the heart of the Dredger beat with expectant pleasure when the loaded dredge is safely landed on the vessel's deck.

He is, we will suppose, on unknown ground. What will he find? Human eye has never penetrated below the surface of these unfished waters; dredge or trawl have never yet revealed the mysteries of life which lie hidden in these virgin submarine abodes. What will he find? Haply some mystic creature believed to have only lived in by-gone ages, some living representative of an extinct fauna!

The sailors term the dredge, the "drudge;" and so, indeed, it is to them, for only the labour is theirs, and no small amount of that, in hauling in the implement of science; the rare delight of viewing with appreciative eye the treasures when first brought to light, is the naturalist's. The pretty sea-stars and the shells with vivid tints are the only strangers in the dredge that claim any notice from the lookers-on; all queer sober crabs, and all muddy amorphous organisms in, for the time being, a quiescent state, are regarded with stolid indifference or with positive dislike. A living fish may give a spasmodic flirt with its tail and excite a moment's interest, or should the claw of a crab fasten on the doctor's finger, there is a gleam of fun, but the transient smile dies away, and the unpopular implement, emptied of its contents, is pitched overboard with something like an imprecation.

But honour to the dredge, say I, rough, unsightly, coarse indeed to view, but a true and dear friend to the seeker after the strange truths that lie hidden at the bottom of the sea.

Unless the mind is prepared by education, minute beauties lie hid from the human eye, and the sailors, who stand around me, gaze at the tub of sandy mud and broken shells, yet all fail to see the delicate lacelike beauty and the fragile elegance of form assumed by the numerous organic creatures which encrust the dull flat stones, and the odd and broken pecten valves which we have fished up with so much labour from the bottom of the sea.

These old dead water-worn shells are seldom altogether worthless, and should never be thrown away without at least a cursory examination. Singular hermit-crabs often take possession of these deserted houses; rare Calyptræ often nestle snugly in the apertures of the univalve kind, while very frequently Serpulæ with highly elaborate tubes covered with charming sculpture coil themselves about the battered ruin. On the flat valves of the bivalves whole colonies of lovely fragile polyzoa may encrust the surface, and little fairy, graceful, living mosses form, like ivy concealing the decaying walls of an ancient ruin, networks and embroideries over their corroded valves.

We had been driven by the fury of the gale through La Pérouse Strait into the sea of Okhotsk, and were again quietly at anchor in Aniwa Bay, in Saghaleen, as the Ainos, the aborigines of the island, call it. It is also termed by the natives, "Isoka;" in fact, I find that geographers as well as naturalists may sometimes be embarrassed by a multiplicity of synonyms. The Japanese call the island "Oku-Yesso;" the Russians "Sachalien;" it is named by old writers, "Karafto;" and in ancient maps it is "Sahalien," "Ula-hata," "Augo-hata," "Island of the Black River," and "Amur." By Siebold, followed by Keith Johnston, it is called "Tarakai," but the name by which it is generally known is "Saghaleen," derived from "Sagarün," one of the names of the Amur River.

The general features of the island are very similar to those of the opposite coast of Manchuria. Primary formations compose hills and rocks of varying heights, and wild tracts of country are covered with high rank grass, scrub, and masses of fine trees. The most conspicuous trees are conifers, pines, yews, and junipers. A kind of dogwood is common, and I observe a beech, an oak, and a species of Euonymus. The aster and pink, a small gentian, the Flower of Yarrow and St. John's-wort, a species of Ribes, and the pretty white-flowered Grass of Parnassus, are among the common plants. A dark Marchantia covers the ground in damp places, in which also a Lycopodium is conspicuous. Of ferns I gathered a species of Pteris and a Polystichum.

As we landed in a shallow bight of the splendid bay, we observed the duck family in full feather. The pretty golden-eye was swimming and diving near the shore, or indulging in little playful flights on and off the land; elegant long-tailed ducks were flying wildly and uttering loud cries; whistling widgeons were passing by in twos and threes; and conspicuous in the bustling noisy crowd were the beautiful shieldrake and the solitary shoveller.

These, with the mallards and the teal, made the shallow waters of the little sandy bays vocal with their quackings and screamings, and it was at once highly exciting and amusing to watch their loves and quarrels, their flutterings, alarms, and greedy gobblings. The little guillemot kept turning gaily about in the water, and the long necks and pointed heads of the divers were seen at intervals above the surface.

At the water's edge the golden plovers and the sand-pipers came trooping along the mud-flats, while the shrill whistle of the oystercatcher and the cry of the curlew were heard in the distance. Half buried in the shingly beach, I observed the huge skull of some hapless whale, stranded in the shallows after having sought shelter in the bay. Just before we landed, we perceived a black bear trotting along the beach. Before he had climbed the red cliff behind him, he was saluted with a rifle ball, which caused him to turn his head and cast an angry glance upon the intruders on his domain. We found the seaweed scratched up by

Bruin, who had been down foraging for shellfish, dead crabs and mollusks being numerous on the sand after the recent gale.

The captain and myself landed, and discovered the abodes of the Ainos, in precisely the same manner as did M. de Langle and his companions in the time of La Pérouse. "They saw a litter of blind puppies, the mother of which, barking in the woods, led them to suppose that the owners were not far off." A half-scared woman, seeing us approach, endeavoured to conceal herself in the tall grass. She was, however, detected, and good-humouredly hunted down, when she made for the door of a little smoke-dried hovel. We followed her, and pushing gently aside the sliding board which served the purpose of a door, we entered smiling, and lo! the entire family was before us. The countenance of the frightened damsel was shrouded by a veil of loose black hair, and all were silent and solemn, squatting on their hams around the fire; gipsy-fashion an iron cauldron, with its seething mess of fish, hung suspended in the midst.

No sign of welcome was made, no peace-offering accepted. We therefore quietly withdrew, and entered another and a larger hut. Here we found four men seated around the smouldering wood fire solemnly smoking, while two young women were clearing away the fish-bones and fragments that remained after the recent meal. The interior of the dingy abode was lined with matting, and on a raised platform on one side were an old woman and some children. The captain and myself seated ourselves among these strange people, and endeavoured to win the hearts of the women by pictures from the "Illustrated London News," which they accepted timidly, and contemplated upside down. The absurd little brown monkey-like imps were regaled with sweet biscuits, which they shyly munched with silent gusto, and the stolid hairy men were propitiated with tobacco, which they sliced up and smoked instanter. We were amused and pleased to note the skilful way in which one little savage lighted his grandmother's pipe, and were surprised to observe that ancient dame, with

MALE AND FEMALE COSTUME. 237

a black mane, crouching on all fours, like some hideous sphinx, begin smoking the soothing weed with apparently the most perfect appreciation of its excellent quality.

The dress of the men of this remote region is composed of coarse canvas or the skins of dogs and seals. Their legs are protected by laced buskins, and their feet by clumsy straw sandals. Every man carries a knife in a wooden sheath, and a carved tobacco pouch. The lips of the women are tattooed of a pale black colour, and their coarse straight hair is neither gathered up in a becoming knot, nor confined by coquettish net or other feminine device, but is simply parted down the middle, and very much resembles a huge black mop. These "unlovely" women have enormous metal ear-rings depending from the lobes of their ears, and necklaces of coloured beads adorn their necks. They are clothed in silver-gray or spotted seal-skins, and wear long boots of the same material reaching above the knee. A black leathern girdle, or "cestus Veneris," encircles their waist, which is covered with brass ornaments, and from which is invariably suspended the all-useful knife. Oysters, mussels, and scallops, mingled with the bones of salmon, seal, and porpoise, are thrown in heaps around their houses, showing their piscivorous propensities, and giving evidence of the debt these poor people owe to the sea. The one idea of their existence seems to be the capture of salmon. These noble fish they sell to the Japanese, "reserving," says La Pérouse, "for themselves only the stench, which adheres to their houses, furniture, clothes, and even the very grass surrounding their villages."

As they come striding through the tall grass, with their bows and spears, and their long hair streaming in the wind, the Ainos give one the idea of being formidable savages; but this ferocious exterior suggests recollections of the ass in the lion's skin, and only serves as a cloak to hide a harmless, timid nature. On suddenly meeting a party in the woods the men crouch down and the women and children "hide their diminished heads."

Their hirsute limbs, long tangled hair, and bushy beards have earned for them the sobriquet of "hairy Kuriles," but on close inspection the general expression of their faces is that of good nature combined with stupidity, a view of their character which is fully borne out by their large heads and clumsy figures.

The Ainos are certainly not the original stock from which the Japanese have sprung, as the two races have little in common, either physically or morally. Their language even is different, being similar to that spoken by the Kuriles. This is the opinion of M. de Rosney, who observes, in his "Introduction to the Study of the Japanese Language," "It was considered very probable that the natives of the islands situated in the seas to the north of Japan might speak an idiom approaching to that of the Japanese, and consequently might belong to the same linguistic family. The study of the Aino language and of the different dialects used in the island of Yesso and the Kuriles, obliges us to consider this opinion as completely inadmissible."

In two respects I observed that these Aino tribes resemble the Aborigines of Formosa, who are called by the Chinese "Tai-lo-kok." Mr. Swinhoe, who saw a few of them, observes that "their hair was short and fringed on the forehead; behind it hung loose." The second peculiarity is the circumstance of their arrows having no feathered shaft, which appears very strange, as birds are abundant, and feathered shafts are generally in vogue among all who habitually use the bow. I do not know if there is any linguistic affinity between these two tribes of wild men. M. de Rosny says, "The Formosan language, or that of Formosa or Taiwan, appears itself to be a branch of the Oceanic family."

CHAPTER XVII.

Hakodadi—Vegetation—Pleasing Aspect of the Scenery—Appearance of the Town—A Temple of Buddha—Visit to the Theatre—The Audience and the Play—Vicinity of the Town—A Charming Retreat—Intercourse with Nature.

On July the 15th we arrived at Hakodadi, which has the aspect of a poor and straggling fishing village, but is very prettily situated at the foot of a long bluff promontory which projects from the southernmost corner of the island of Yesso. The lower portions of the hills have some fine groves of dark fir-trees, and the upper part is clothed with brushwood. In some places paths have been formed through the groves, and here and there a little garden is cultivated. The summit is bare, barren, brown, and rocky.

The vegetation of the island is very similar to that of the opposite coast of Manchuria. Many of the plants are of the same species. The homely dandelion is here, with the familiar jagged leaves; and we gathered the spikes of Plantago media for our canaries. The lily of the valley, in her modest robes of white and green, is growing in profusion, and on the sandy soil the gay Calystegia Soldanella is flaunting in all her finery. The Chinese pink grows beside the shepherd's-purse, and the Trollius japonicus mingles her yellow flowers with the golden cups of Caltha palustris. The Japanese day-lily vies with the Iris japonica. The bee-haunted blooms of Stephanandra flexuosa are seen in the swampy plains; and in many parts the eye is gladdened with roses, celandines, honeysuckles, and anemones. The entire scenery, so lavishly variegated with flowers, is very pleasing to those who have recently left the barren rounded hills of Northern China, or the green sameness of the rice-fields in the South.

On entering the town the impression produced is equally agreeable, the quiet and order which everywhere prevail contrasting so remarkably with the noise, dirt, and confusion of Chinese cities. There is here no tumult in the streets; but the craftsmen are busy in their shops. Smiling damsels are drawing water at the wells, and even the children are demure and well behaved, no unruly urchins throwing dirt at the stranger as he passes. The very dogs have a sort of canine politeness, and disdain to snarl and bark at the wanderer from distant climes who has landed on their shore. The streets are wide, well watered, and bounded by rows of unpainted houses consisting of one story, each offering on the roof the somewhat remarkable spectacle of a tub of water and a broom, obviously precautions in case of fire.

As I strolled alone about the town I came to the great temple of Buddha, into the courts of which I entered. It was ornamented with numerous strange devices, among which were quaint dragons and huge stone tortoises. While I was gazing abstractedly at these ungainly figures, a burst of sunlight streaming through a little window in the roof covered the colossal gilded idol with a golden glory, revealing at the same time the figure of a female devotee prostrate on her face before the shrine. The temple gardens are in a solemn pine-wood, and the central avenue is ornamented with grand solid monoliths sacred to the dead. Not the least remarkable objects are the ancient sculptured rock-masses covered with inscriptions. As I was examining them, the solemn tones of the great bell ringing out from a wooden tower in a corner of the sacred grove filled me with a feeling of awe which I could easily account for.

During our sojourn at Hakodadi we made up a little party, and went to the theatre, which, on entering, we found to be a large, dimly-lighted, and barn-like house, with a roomy elevated stage, but with no scenery or orchestra, in which respect it differed from some of the theatres at Yeddo and Osaca, in which there is an orchestra, the musicians forming it playing on gongs suspended from a frame-work, kettledrums, and a few wind instruments similar to flageolets and fifes.

As we entered the building we paid at the door, and were very politely escorted to a row of raised seats at the side of the stage, which represented the boxes.

The body of the house was filled with a motley throng of delighted spectators, sitting on benches arranged as in the pit of our own play-houses. In some of the theatres, as shown by a representation of one in my Japanese books, the pressure of the crowd in the pit is regulated in a very ingenious manner, the entire area being filled with a network of barricades, each compartment occupied by from four to six spectators. In this picture, moreover, there are boxes and galleries, and the stage is filled with numerous actors arrayed in gorgeous and fantastic costumes.

The play was going on, and we knew not how long it had been "dragging its slow length along," because one play often lasts for several days, and several plays go on in rotation. This allows the spectator of any particular play opportunities for leaving to partake of refreshment. Smoking went on without intermission during the performance, and innumerable little cups of saki were handed round amid great general hilarity. As far as I could understand what I saw on the stage, two hired assassins or lonins entered, disguised, and stole the child of some great Daimio. The mother appeared just in time to witness the unexpected abduction of her darling. Indignant and distracted, she was carried out in a demented state, with dishevelled hair, by her distressed young handmaidens. The two conspirators again appeared with the unhappy child, whom they barbarously murdered before our eyes, the blood flowing freely from—a pig's bladder, hid artfully from view. The acting of the boy representing the dying child was perfectly marvellous. He stretched out his little limbs, moaned, gasped, became faint, and finally closed his eyes and died, producing as painful a sensation as the deformed man in the play of the Colleen Bawn.

At this juncture the bereaved mother again appeared, looking anxiously around with wild eyes and clasped hands. Perceiving her child lying upon the ground, she leant over him, snatched him up in her arms, and clasped him to her breast. Her agony was admirably expressed; and the better to enable the spectators to observe the play of her features, a man crawled about in front of the stage with a long pole, bearing at the end a light with which he illumined the countenance of the actress.

In the next act, which did not appear to have any reference to the foregoing, we were astonished to see the frightful ceremony of the Hara-Kiri turned into ridicule. The chief actor in this comedy of the by-no-means-to-be-laughed-at "happy despatch" or honourable suicide, was a well-dressed noble of portly bearing, with a rubicund and jolly countenance. For some offence, to us unknown, he had been ordered by the Tycoon to kill himself. Surrounded by his sorrowing friends and relatives, and, as is usual, his dearest friend ready with his sword to strike off his head, he prepares for the fearful act; but no sooner does he feel the sharp edge of his sword than he shrinks from the contemplation of the suicidal act, making comic grimaces, to the intense delight of the spectators of both sexes, who scream with merriment, and applaud him most vociferously.

The immediate vicinity of Hakodadi is very pretty, and surburban villas, with pretty gardens, are very numerous. I came across one of these charming retreats, where a party of elderly gentlemen were amusing themselves with a bow and arrow. They discharged their arrows in a kneeling posture, and seemed highly delighted when they hit the bull's-eye. They invited me in, and treated me with the utmost politeness. I reposed on handsome mats, and with my entertainers was served by pages who offered us little cups of tea and saki, after which we smoked. As we were ignorant of each other's language, we could only converse very unsatisfactorily by signs. In the course of my ramble I also came across another party. These were out taking the air, and were also attended by pages carrying refreshments, mats, and even camp-stools. They accosted me with great courtesy, examined my sweeping-net and collecting bottle, and pressed me to partake of a pipe, and a tiny measure of pink scented saki. In fact, nothing could exceed the courteous politeness and the generous hospitality of the natives of this place.

On returning to the ship, I had the satisfaction of seeing one of those interminable processions of followers belonging to some neighbouring Kami or Daimio. It was both a novel and imposing sight. The horses were richly caparisoned, and covered with showy, embroidered trappings; footmen bore aloft numerous quaint emblems, and banners with elaborate devices; two-sworded men swaggered with great state among the showy throng, inflated, apparently, with an overweening consciousness of their own dignity and importance.

While rambling in the streets my attention was particularly directed to two mysterious creatures with their heads concealed in huge bee-hive like helmets, who were playing dismal tunes on bamboo flageolets. These I was told were begging priests, who wander from door to door, doleful, dreary, and blindfold, soliciting alms. I was much pleased with the groups of small shaven-pated children, in long cotton gowns, whose acquaintance I soon made, though they were a little shy at first. They gathered wild flowers as I passed along, and gleefully presented them to me, reminding me of a similar custom I had observed in Wales.

*　　*　　*　　*　　*

After our return to Hakodadi, a few days of monotonous routine on board a ship made me desirous of renewing my acquaintance with the shore. As the day was fine and tempting I took my course along the wide sweeping curve round Hakodadi Bay. Long strings of horses, carrying all kinds of merchandise, passed me repeatedly. I bought a wicker-basket for an "itzebu," and filled it with skulls and shells before I got afloat again. I intended to cross the narrow sandy isthmus connecting the two bays, and follow the outline of the outer one. I wandered far along the sandy beach, my soothing pipe inviting meditation. My eyes, that "to their earthy mother tended," were intent on chalcedony, carnelians, and nodules of marble, of which there are galore, on the "beached margent of the sea." I passed the sunken camp where astute Nipong men daily practise rifle-shooting, and near which there are tempting deposits that invite inspection, rewarding the coleopterist sometimes with a huge black shard-beetle, an amethystine species, and a singular kind with a long recurved frontal horn, and where green chaffers abound on the leaves of the young oaks. Vast mounts of white sand, covered with undulations like the ripples of the sea; drift-hillocks, soft and dazzling like heaps of snow; long wavy ridges, half burying the fishermen's huts, and banking up the boat-houses, are seen on every side. Nature presents all her beauties in rich profusion. The roses are large, blushing, and fragrant, and the Sedums with their whorled succulent green leaves, invite the eye. Rolling down the gentle sand declivities, or crawling painfully up the banks, under the dry, scattered shards of oxen and horses, under heaps of dead leaves, and by the snaky roots of brine-washed plants, there nestle scores and scores of gray-brown, rusty, brown-black, rough-coated indolent Opatrums, or sand-beetles. Without much labour one may gather them by bushels, and leave as many for his friends. With the exception of their colour, which varies according to the amount of sand and dirt on their bodies, they are all alike as two peas, and tired, dusty, and ungrateful, one comes to the conclusion that all is—Opatrums and sand.

CHAPTER XVIII.

Beautiful Tsu-Sima—Mussel Cove and Oyster Sound—The Adela Moth—Paulownia Imperialis—Fossil Trees—Capture of a Damaster—Gigantic Oysters—Island of Sado—Shooting Party—Taxus Fruit—Diard's Pheasant—Nisi Bama—Singular Spectacle—Squid Fishing—Squid Village—An Odd Fish.

CONTINUING our explorations, we next proceeded to Tsu-Sima, which is cut up into deep sounds and bays with a rocky bottom, and in these again are numerous snug little coves and sheltered basins. Two of these are set down in our chart as Mussel Cove and Oyster Sound, names given by us on account of the shell-fish they so liberally supply. A boat-load of mussels gave every man in the ship about two pounds of mussel-meat, the flesh of each mussel averaging four ounces. The oysters, however, are more attractive, and we determined to make up a party in order to seek out and enjoy these delectable "natives" in a free "al fresco" style.

The finest being on the opposite side of the island, we had to make our way to them overland. We proceeded, accordingly, through groves of dark clustering Cryptomerias and tangled bushes of yellow-fruited raspberries. Our course was partly along the scooped-out rugged banks of an old shallow, rocky watercourse, where the trout were seen leaping after flies, and where ugly bull-headed fish were dimly discerned deep down in clear dark pools between the rounded boulders. Sometimes we had to pick our way through patches of peas and barley, and over fields of sweet potatoes, gathering as we proceeded the sweet-scented flowers of Syringa. We were struck with the vast numbers of a species of sun-beetle which we perceived clinging to the flowers of the Japanese privet. I stopped to gaze, with admiration and delight, on an elegant little moth called Adela, with striped golden wings and long vibrating antennæ; I secured a bee-like, hairy Trichius, or flower-beetle, buried deep in the bosom of a purple thistle; and numerous large Elaters, or snap-beetles, flying in the sun with bodies vertical and horizontal wings, also fell victims to my predatory predilections. I discovered some specimens of the Helivingia ruscifolia, a singular little plant described by Siebold, and I secured a few fronds of the glorious fern, Anemia ternata, which flowers in the same manner as the Osmund Royal.

Proceeding on our journey, we ascended the gully, still following the course of the tumbling burn which flowed along the bottom. Above and around, clumps of light green oaks were mingled with sombre-spreading fir-trees, with occasional patches of elder, and here and there with soft, billowy clusters of Cryptomeria japonica. Impending overhead were grey slate-stone rocks peeping out from among the trees, while high aloft, conspicuous by her gorgeous head of crowded fox-glove blossoms, towered the Paulownia Imperialis—truly a sylvan queen. Another curious pale broad nebula in the sea of green was caused by thousands of upturned bracts of Benthamia japonica.

As we emerged suddenly from our bowery chasm

we encountered quite a different scene. In the bight of a sheltered bay lay the brown thatched houses of a village. The sea was clear and calm, and the sun shone bright on the wooded hills on the opposite side of the Sound. Some slender sharp-prowed boats, propelled by bare-headed islanders clothed in blue, reminded us we were now among the people of the "Land of the Rising Sun."

Next afternoon we took the gig and pulled up the intricate Sound until we were attracted by a deep circular little bay, entirely surrounded by towering trees, extending as far as the steep and rocky shore. On the precipitous banks huge fragments and stumps of what seemed to us fossil-trees abounded, the softer rock in which they were embedded having been washed away by the rain and the tide.

As for the oysters, their number and size astonished and delighted us. Some specimens were truly gigantic, the flesh of one alone actually weighing twelve ounces. We found them rather deep down, adhering to the sides of rock-basins, filled with the clearest water, pure as crystal. The rocks were weed-grown with feathery dulse and broad-leaved tangle, and abounded in large-eared sea-hares and delicate-tinted sea-slugs.

I had the good fortune, on this occasion, to make what I considered a great capture, that namely of a Damaster! But what is a Damaster, my readers may inquire. It is Fortune's beetle—an insect much desired by entomologists. I was walking alone at the time, for all hands had gone on board to dinner, along the shell-strewn strand of Tabu-Sima, a charming little island not far from the shores of Niphon. I was in a brown study, smoking a little clay pipe, and thinking chiefly of the contempt in which I should be held if some of my "very respectable friends" saw me in my disreputable "rig," for my neck was bare, my coat was an old blue serge, and as for my hat it was brown felt, and I must say "a shocking bad one." However, the sun was bright, the clear blue rippling sea was calm, the little island was new and verdurous, and I smoked serenely. On a sudden my abstract downward gaze encountered a grotesque Coleopteron in a suit of black, stalking slowly and deliberately among the drift-wood at my feet, stepping cautiously and delicately over the "spillican" twigs, like a Catholic priest in a crowded thoroughfare. At once I knew my coleopterous acquaintance to be Damaster, so I carefully lifted my unresisting sable friend from his native soil, and after giving him a good long stare, I deposited him in a bottle. From his name and appearance I judged him to be cousin to Blaps, and I turned over the rock-weed for his brothers and other relations, but though Helops was there, Damaster was not. Puzzled, but not baffled, I conceived his tastes might be more particular, so I ascended the steep green sides of the island and cast about for rotten trees, nor was I long in discovering a very promising stump, nicely decayed, and full of holes enough to captivate the heart of any beetle. Being, however, fatigued with my scansorial efforts, I sat down before the citadel of the Damaster, and assisted my deliberations by smoking a solemn pipe! Having propitiated Nicotiana and matured my plan of operations, I commenced the work of destruction, when lo! among the vegetable *débris* I descried a long dusky leg, anon two more, and then, buried among the ruins, the struggling Damaster.

Nearly opposite Niegata, in Niphon, one of the new ports of Japan very shortly to be opened to Europeans, there is a very beautiful island with a rocky iron-bound coast certainly, but the interior of which abounds in green trees and wooded hills, which are separated by deep gullies, gradually expanding in their turn into rich alluvial plains watered by rivulets, and parcelled off into productive padi-fields. The name of this little island is Sado, and here it was that I formed one of a party which was bent on the shooting of pheasants.

At first our way was by the sea-shore, over great level plains of rock, which seemed as if they had once boiled and been covered with bubbles of stone, which, having burst, had left circular hollows with raised edges. Here we found plenty of chitons, a cuttle or so, whelks in abundance, a few queer crabs, but—as yet no pheasants. Anon we wandered by the weed-grown margin of a shallow stream, which sparkled, eddied, and went on its way rejoicing, forming in its course numerous little waterfalls. By its side ran, and flirted up and down, the tricksy water-ouzel, often making a dash into the small shallow rapids. Here also were the mild slender wagtails, yellow, pied, and gray. Very impudent rooks were perched on every tree, and the noisy jays were flirting violently among the branches of the oaks. But—we saw no pheasants. We followed the upward course of the mountain-stream, and were gradually shut in by the sides of a very charming valley. Bright yellow Persimons hung, like the golden fruit of the Hesperides, on leafless trees; dark spreading yews harboured within their cool shade snug little cottages, and on every side, to the eye's delight, were tapering soft elegant Cryptomerias, mingled with broad-leaved sycamores, and the magnificent foliage of oaks and chestnuts.

Desirous of procuring a few acorns we stooped to

gather some under the trees, and our occupation being observed, a good-natured Japanese ran into his house and brought out handfuls of a nut, very similar in appearance to that which we were picking up, but which we recognised as the kernel of a species of Taxus growing around. These we were requested to eat, and amid much merriment at our expense, in making so absurd a mistake, our acorns were treated with pantomimic abhorrence and disgust. The Taxus fruit had been boiled in salt and water and was pretty tolerable, though rather rough to the palate. But the pheasants? Well, leaving me to "moon" about as usual, my impulsive messmate, Lieutenant Warren, a sportsman, successful as well as enthusiastic, struck across the country, and very soon saw ten or eleven pheasants feeding together in the open spaces of the scrub. They were first recognised by the peculiar short crow common to the pheasant family, and were by no means shy, never having seen sportsmen before. Their favourite haunt seemed to be in the shrubs and high grass on the rising land between the cultivated fields. These pheasants are the rare and lovely Phasianus versicolor, or Diard's pheasant, found only in Japan. "It would be difficult," exclaimed my friend, elated as was natural, "to describe my sensations when first startled by the metallic splendour of the plumage of this king of pheasants. But," continued he, "if the sportsman wishes to 'make a bag,' he must be prepared for a hard day's work, for the ground is very hilly and irregular."

Three brace and a half fell this day to the excellent shooting of Lieutenant Warren. At a dinner given on board Diard's pheasant formed a conspicuous feature, and the flesh was pronounced quite equal to that of his English congener.

On the 19th November we arrived late in the evening off Nisi-Bama, in the Oki Islands, a very charming little group not far from the shores of Niphon. As we neared the anchorage the lights on the water were so numerous and brilliant, and all moving about in such an exceedingly *ignis fatuus* kind of manner that a boat was sent with the interpreter to ascertain the cause of such an unusual spectacle. On his return "Oudah" reported that the maritime will-o'-the-wisps belonged to fishing-boats, hundreds of which, he said, were out looking for "Ika-Surame," an appellation which, after some circumlocution, and many elaborate attempts at explanation, we ascertained meant simply "squids." The lights were produced by birch-bark, kindled in small kinds of gratings with long wooden handles, machines known among seafaring men by the name of "devils." The flame of the fires is very clear and vivid, and the "devils" are held over the boats to attract the squids. These, I find, are a species of Ommastrephes, a sort of sea-cuttle, which is nocturnal in its habits, and which swims very rapidly near the surface in immense shoals. They are taken by a method which is known among fishermen as "jigging." The "jig" is made of iron, and consists of a long shank surmounted by a circlet of small recurved hooks. These cuttles are famous articles of diet both with the Japanese and Chinese, and are carefully dried for the market, where they are sold in vast quantities. They are also extensively used as bait in fishing for bonito and other large fish of the mackerel tribe, which abound along the coasts. The squid is strung through its entire length, the club of one of the long tentacular arms artfully covering and concealing the hook.

Near Hakodadi there is a small fishing village exclusively devoted to the capture and curing of these nutritious Cephalopods. Many hundreds of thousands may here be daily seen drying in the open air, suspended in regular rows on lines, which are raised on poles about six feet from the ground, all very nicely cleaned and kept flat by means of bamboo stretchers. The open spaces are filled with these squid-laden lines, and before all the houses in the village squids everywhere form a novel kind of screen. The Japanese name of the place is Shai-Sawabi, but by us it was always called "Squid village."

On the 20th, I landed with the captain at the village of Nisi-Bama. The valleys between the steep wooded hills were very curiously cultivated in terraces, causing them to resemble so many verdant amphitheatres. We passed through a wicket, ascended a steep path through a grove of fine trees, and found it led to the trunk of a gigantic bastard-banyan or Ficus nitida, evidently a sacred tree, for the base was covered with paper effigies and other votive offerings, and a little gaudy joss was discovered squatting in a niche. On regaining the village we found the people very civil, though rather in awe of the foreigners, possibly the first of our race they had ever seen. Their houses were neatly built, with tiled roofs, and with comfortable sheds for horses, cows, and pigs. Dried squids abounded, and from the projecting rafters of a gable-end I observed a grotesque-looking dried shark's head, evidently the trophy of adventurous fishermen. Entering the abode so decorated, I encountered an aged crone pounding the daily rice. She was inclined to be in a rage at my intrusion, but displaying in my manner as much of the "suaviter in modo" as possible, I effected the purchase of the architectural ornament for the small sum of one itzebu.

This "squaline caput" is sufficiently bizarre to merit observation. It has been inspected by many a seafaring man, from an admiral to a powder-monkey, and its physiognomy, though sufficiently striking, is unknown even to a class usually well-acquainted with the tribe in question. The head, which is narrow and somewhat compressed, is covered with a smooth black skin; the snout is long, triangular, and pointed, not depressed, and projects considerably over the mouth, which is open with a wide gape; the gums are exposed and painted red. The eye is large and round, and unprovided with a nictitating membrane or eyelid. The nostrils are oblique, ear-like openings placed at the lower part of the muzzle, midway between its tip and the eye. The teeth are arranged in three series, the outer row erect, the middle semi-erect, and the inner decumbent; they are similar in each jaw, and are long, pointed, curved cusps, with their lateral edges sharp and simple.

CHAPTER XIX.

Nagasaki—The Scenery—Vegetation—Insect Life—The Woodcutter—The Harbour—Desima and Pappenberg—State Barge and Pleasure Boats—Scenes in the Streets—Mendicant Priest—A Bonze—Strolling Acrobats—Cemeteries—Ceremonies in Honour of the Dead—The Temples—Dog-Fancier's Shop—Gigantic Salamanders—Fish Festival—A Ramble in Kiusiu.

We next proceeded to the south of the island of Kiusiu, and landed at Nagasaki. The first time I went ashore I ascended the hill on the right of the harbour, through fields of ground-nuts and bearded wheat. The grassy banks, which form the boundaries of the land, are planted at intervals with elegant wax trees, which are often garlanded with cissus-vines and ivy. Among the loose stones glides the slender blue-tailed lizard; and the abundant red fruit of a species of Potentilla offers a sorry substitute for the strawberry. My road lay in a sunken rocky path, over-arched with trees, like some of the North Devon lanes. Among the dead leaves on the ground, I captured specimens of a very fine carabus, and as I emerged once more from this shady path into the merry sunshine, I saw apoderus, hispa, and cassida alighting on the sunlit leaves. At this season of the year there are but few flowers, but you will notice everywhere the white clustering blossoms of Syringa, the white dog-rose, and the welcome fragrant honeysuckle.

When I reached the pine-clad summit of the hill all appeared silent and solemn. The only bird I saw was a large kite, which hovered above the trees, and the only sound I heard was the continuous cawing of the rooks and the loud grating noise of the cicada. The hills of Tsu-Sima are composed of slate-stone, and in that island, among the loose moss-grown stones among the trees, I discovered several kinds of air-breathing mollusks; but here the basis of the hills is granite, and I cannot find a single species of operculate land shell. Among the foliage of the trees I noticed Hadra orientalis, a handsome banded snail, and Hadra peliomphala. In the dense brushwood on earthy banks, I found

Satsuma japonica, and the common Acusta Sieboldi. With the exception of some dark-winged butterflies, insect life seemed very scarce. The flat stones even, on being turned, revealed nothing but wood-lice, centipedes, and cymatiæ. A small yelping cur detected me in the act of transporting some bundles of brushwood in search of snails, and anon, his owner, a broad-faced, smiling Caliban, appeared. The honest wood-cutter was even more astonished at my voluntary labour than his "friend on all fours," but muttering "moosi," which means "creeping things," he rattled a bit of chain, saying interrogatively, "Ma?" which being interpreted, signifies, "Have you seen my pony pass this way?" I shook my head, and pointing to my collecting-bottle, repeated "Esha." On this hint—for Esha means "Doctor" —I was treated with profound respect, and the old peasant, suddenly vanishing into the bush, speedily returned with both hands filled with beetles. By the use of three words only, we had succeeded in understanding each other.

From my elevated position in the fir-clearing I

now looked down upon the land-locked harbour. To the right is Desima, and to the left is Pappenberg, down whose steep sides it is said fifteen thousand Christians were once precipitated. All around green wooded hills, checkered with fields of yellow wheat, rise up from the water's edge. The dark smooth surface of the harbour was dotted with strange-fashioned craft. The monotonous cries of the boatmen, "Ush-shia, ush-shia," faintly reached my ear, as, bending to their powerful sculls, these semi-nude athletes urged their sharp-prowed boats swiftly through the water. Parties of women sang gaily as they crossed in boats from shore to shore; fishing-boats were casting their nets, while clean unpainted trading junks spread their white sails to the favouring breeze; and the dark banner-bearing barge of the Japanese governor, propelled by many oars, and looking like a galley of old Rome, moved with slow and solemn state to the sound of music.

The long wide streets of Nagasaki are sometimes very gay, especially on festive occasions, or in the evening when the labours of the day are over, and the genial time has arrived when, as our Interpreter Tatish would say, they "talk nonsense and drink saki." At such periods, a motley throng is seen. I may notice some of the natives that came under my own observation, trooping along the narrow side paths.

First, there was a party of three who met in the middle of the road, and their three broad circular hats, seen from a distance, appeared to take the form of a gigantic shamrock, as they bowed their heads together. Next, a tipsy samourai, or government official, swaggered past me, with the straight hilts of his swords projecting half-a-foot in front of his protuberant abdomen. He was followed by a timid mother leading a little child, their gentle aspect forming quite a contrast to the braggadocio air of the drunken yakonin. A row of half-naked coolies trotted rapidly along in single file, bending under heavy baskets, which were borne at the ends of the bamboos across their shoulders. In the middle of the street, a lady in a norimon was carried at a swinging even pace by two stalwart bearers. Three more norimons came after, followed by that more plebeian conveyance, a cango. In the centre of the road, was a lean small horse holding down his head, and led by a decrepit old man; while a fatter horse was surmounted by a stoutish man in a conical hat, who sat perched up on a mountain of merchandise.

On the side path we nearly ran against a vendor of sweetmeats, ringing a little bell like our muffin-man, and praising the quality of his wares with the voice of a stentor; a man with a shiny black paper hat, who followed him, was, I learned on inquiry, a priest of the Kami sect; while two gentlemen, whom I observed on the other side of the street, in their petticoat trowsers or nakamas, were about to pay a visit of ceremony. Their attention, I saw, was attracted by two laughing girls, with vermilion lips and faces white with paint, who were undoubtedly "up to mischief." An odd-looking figure, who came stalking along, striking his stick, which was furnished with jangling metal rings, upon the pavement, was pointed out to me as a mendicant priest;

and a man with a bare smooth shaven head, I was informed, was a bonze of the Buddhist order. I was much amused by the appearance of a little boy, who came carelessly along, having positively nothing on him but a very large saucer-shaped yellow hat; and a coolie, who was groaning and perspiring under the weight of two enormous boxes, was scarcely more amply clad. A few friends, who had met in the middle of the road, were gently bending, rubbing their knees and sucking in their breath to express their mutual high regard. But who are these that come careering down the road, with a noisy din of gongs, and fifes, and drums? It is a troupe of strolling acrobats, who will shortly be seen lying on their backs, and balancing ladders on the soles of their feet; causing their paper butterflies to flirt and flutter in the air; or spinning tops which, with wonderful dexterity, are made to run along the edge of a sword.

There then passed us, in rapid succession, a sedate but needy-looking man with a huge bundle of sticks slung across his back; a barber with his shaving apparatus; a coolie staggering under the weight of two earthenware pots; a young man with a lantern at the end of a long stick; a policeman with a checkered robe; a pretty woman with a little dog in her arms; and a blind beggar chanting dolorously. In front of the bath-houses were merry groups of both sexes, some placidly smoking, others making love, a few telling stories, and the rest staring vacantly about them. A cross-grained old man looked very vicious while chopping off the head of a very ugly fish, the wickedness of his aspect contrasting with the mild manner of a decidedly stout party seated behind his little store of fruit, and sheltered from the heat by a gigantic paper umbrella. A kindly-looking father showed that he was quite a domestic man by the manner in which he carried his little daughter on his head; while a traveller beside him, with his nose tied up, stepped along more independently with a goodly pack upon his back. A well-dressed beau showed how anxious he was to preserve the delicacy of his complexion by carefully shading his face with his outspread fan; and an old man, with spectacles on nose, who, accompanied by two timid shrinking girls, was carrying his umbrella over his shoulder like a sword, gave him a look of cynical contempt as he passed him.

I was much struck by the very cheerful and even gay aspect of the cemeteries of this peculiar people. These cities of the dead are usually situated near the living city, in most picturesque localities, and are planted with clusters of camellia and hibiscus trees. We entered one, and strolled up the noble avenue of fir trees, tall, sombre, and funereal. The great gong in the belfry of the temple had just been sounded, exciting in our minds a feeling of awe, combined with a sentiment of respect for the sacred "Dead." All around us were placed enormous blocks of unhewn granite, arranged with an eye to the picturesque, and having one side smoothed for the name of the departed. We noticed many four-sided monuments, and one with a four-sided conical apex. There were also tablets with semicircular tops, like our ordinary tombstones, and even here and there some elaborately sculptured cenotaphs.

I used to fancy the cemetery at Kensal Green picturesque and pretty, but the old graveyard at Nagasaki is far more attractive. The ground is hilly, and portions have been formed out of the solid rock. The family graves are decked with living flowers, the use of *immortelles* appearing to be unknown. At certain times, we are told, the tombs are lighted up with particoloured lanterns, in honour of the dead, and the relatives hold a mysterious kind of carousal with the spirits of the departed; at other times, groups of young people spend hours kneeling before the decorated shrines of their relatives, or wander cheerfully among the flower-strewn avenues.

The temples dedicated to the worship of their deities, are vast and dingy buildings abounding in hideous idols. These vary in their form and fashion according to the nature and character of the beings they are supposed to represent. The majority, however, are either immense gilt or bronze images of

Buddha, or grotesque and ugly monsters with dragons' heads. The images of the gods of rain and tempest are frightful, and nothing can be more monstrous than some of the masks with goggle eyes and round, bloated cheeks.

The educated classes of the Japanese only smile at the extravagances of the popular religion, looking with contempt on these horrid effigies and mystical imaginary beings. The more intelligent of them prefer the religion of the Kami, or Happy Spirits, a quaint, fantastic form of worship, somewhat similar, I imagine, to the mythology of the Greeks and Romans. Many of them are followers of Confucius, and acknowledge one Great and Supreme Being.

One of the most curious sights in Nagasaki is the dog-fancier's shop, where the far-famed little poodles are sold. You enter a large apartment, where, under the care of a young and handsome woman, are specimens of the canine species of all ages, from the blind struggling puppy to the dog of elderly and respectable appearance. The dog-fancier's wife, who had a sick poodle in her arms, said to me, "I have no children, and so I tend and care for these small dogs," for they are all of the same diminutive breed. It is a singular fact, but they thrive best upon hard dried salmon, which is carefully scraped for them by their kind mistress. There were more than forty dogs in her keeping, and she informed me that last year she lost thirty at one time from influenza.

The song birds in the shop are also very pretty, as are the nuthatches, which are kept in very tall cages, with an upright stick in the middle, at the top of which is a cross-piece with a notch, in which the bird places the nut or berry, which he hews with his pick-like bill till he gets at the kernel. Instead of the more yielding fruit of the yew, which is the usual food of the nuthatch of Japan, at one time I substituted hard hazel-nuts. As the bird was unable to crack these, he placed them one by one in his water-glass, evidently with the notion that they would in time become softer—an interesting proof of intelligence on the part of these birds.

SALAMANDERS.

Here also I saw several fine specimens of Sieboldia maxima, the gigantic salamander of Japan. They are kept in large dark tanks, and are as ugly reptiles as can be well imagined; black sluggish creatures with warty skins, flat heads, no eyes worth mentioning, blunt noses, and short sprawling legs. They are said to come from the mountain streams of Kiusiu, but in reality they are from the neighbourhood of Osaca in Niphon. The only kind of salamander I saw in the shallow streams which are numerous about Nagasaki was the little dingy triton, with an orange-mottled belly, very similar to the water-newt of Europe.

I bought a couple of Sieboldias for the captain, and had them conveyed on board, with a plentiful supply of small live eels for their maintenance during their voyage to England. One of these creatures died in the transit, and his bones are now in my museum; the other, I believe, is still to be seen, the "admired of all admirers," in the reptile-room of the Zoological Gardens. When they had consumed all the eels, small pieces of raw meat were given them, and really, in their purblind way, they seemed to relish them as much as they did their slippery living prey.

One of the sailors, when exhibiting them to his gaping companions, incautiously handled the big one, which, obviously indignant, turned suddenly, and severely lacerated his hand. His comrades, believing the wound to be dangerous, for they imagine these reptiles to be very venomous, showed great sympathy for him in his calamity, but beyond the temporary inconvenience, no serious consequence resulted.

Simonoseki is charmingly situated at the entrance of the Inland Sea. It consists of a single street nearly two miles long, stretched at the base of the steep, low, thickly-wooded hills which extend along the shore of this portion of Niphon. As we approached the town, sounds of wild music greeted the ear, and as we anchored within a stone's throw of the houses, a novel and attractive scene was presented to our view. The quaint and cleanly houses were gaily decorated with flags and many-coloured streamers, mingled everywhere with fantastic devices of odd-shaped fishes, great-eyed, long-armed cuttles, and sea-monsters of "questionable shape." Drums and trumpets were sounding, and the hum of a thousand voices added to the exciting din. The pleased and pleasure-loving Japanese, full of curiosity, swarmed to see the stranger-ship; the town was in a ferment. The windows were filled with women's heads, the quays and landing-places crowded with gaping men and boys. Our arrival, however, was not the cause for so much jubilation. —It was a Fish-festival.

The next day we changed our anchorage, and anchored on the opposite side of the straits, off the little village of Mosi or Mososaki. I landed, and ascending a rocky winding path, came to a charming little temple, with a queer pointed high-peaked roof, where I could look out upon the waters of the Suwo-Nada, the largest division of the Inland Sea, being nearly sixty miles in length.

As I continued my ramble in this pretty corner of Kiusiu, I found many handsome snails, and some smaller but more singular molluscous creatures. I arrived in a short time at the shores of the Seto-Uchi itself, and had an opportunity of examining the vast, shallow, square enclosures where salt is made first by evaporation, and afterwards by boiling down in huge copper pans. I was also greatly interested in an establishment for forging iron, and especially for the manufacture of nails.

Encountering an old man and a child, I soon made their acquaintance, and was invited by them to enter a picturesque cottage, where I had a smoke and some tea with grandpapa, who showed me, with much pride, his chrysanthemums and bantams, the former of gigantic proportions, and the latter perfect little beauties. The old man pointed to the tails of the small strutting cocks, which curled quite over their heads, and were considered the acme of perfection. The Japanese are famous hands at producing odd varieties of plants and animals. They will present you, at will, with a pigeon all white, with a black head and wings, or all black with a white head and wings. A cockscomb shall, with them, be straight or curly, a chrysanthemum be dwarfed or gigantic, a tree be reduced to a tiny shrub. As to the foliage of plants, we all know the spotted and variegated leaves brought home by Veitch and Fortune.

On emerging upon the sandy shore again, my attention was attracted by a dozen women beating-out and winnowing their stores of wheat, which they did in a very ingenious way. Noticing huge flights of steps under wide-spread umbrageous fir and other trees, I ascended them, and came to an ancient joss-house, where were idols more hideous than the most horrid forms which the mind. conceives in nightmare.

CHAPTER XX.

The Seto-Uchi, or Inland Sea—Tomo—Gay Spectacle—The Temple—Tea-house in the Suburb—Priest and Dancing Girls—Women of Japan—The Niphon Belle at Home—Female Costume—Strange Fashions—House of a Wealthy Man of Tomo—Saki Distilleries—Yokohama—Curiosity-Shops—Beautiful Carvings—Japanese Contrasts—The Naruto or Whirlpool.

WHEN we entered the Seto-Uchi—the Inland Sea, the great water highway of Japan—by the Kino Channel, we were immediately struck by the signs of native industry, the number of trading junks, the fertile appearance of the islands, and their numerous population. These indications of commercial prosperity and activity are observed throughout the whole length of the Sea, which is two hundred and forty miles. We noted the tree-crowned summit of Kasaneyama, and the white quartz cliffs of Tsakahara, the palace of the Daimio Hida on the banks of the river which waters the plain about Wakayama and the low, wooded coast of Noma-Sima.

On entering the Idsuma-Nada, we found it free from islands or rocks of any kind. The Seto-Uchi, however, becomes very narrow at Akasi Strait, being there only two miles wide. As the stranger-ship passed quietly along, within a stone's throw of their houses, a blue-robed bare-headed multitude gazed with eager eyes upon us.

In the Bingo-Nada, the high rugged peak of Dotensan's sacred mountain was before us; and the fine cone of Odutsi, nine hundred feet high, was passed. Numerous islands with rounded peaks, most of them cultivated to their very summits, with picturesque villages in sheltered bays, and temples and tea-houses perched on wooded knolls, formed, as the ship glided by, a panorama of as much interest as beauty.

On the north shore lies Tomo, a large town famous for its saki distilleries. Escorted by Araki, our courteous Japanese, the captain and myself landed at a stone pier in the little harbour. It was a period of festival, and all Tomo was alive and out of doors. Gay pennons fluttered from the windows, and wild music was heard in the streets.

Laughter-loving women and smiling graceful girls, clad in scanty narrow skirts, and with huge bows tied behind, were out enjoying themselves. Merry dark-eyed children were in an ecstasy of delight. Strutting, swaggering Yakomins, sword-bearing gentlemen clad in quiet silks, tradesmen in checkered cotton gowns, and serfs bedizened with the badges of their masters, were trooping pleasantly along. Lounging in the doorways were idle matrons; less attractive than the younger daughters of Japan, they were laughing behind their hands to conceal their blackened teeth. Groups of elderly men sat serenely smoking, or sipping saki in their houses. Itinerant vendors of cakes and sweetmeats went about proclaiming the merits of their wares; and brawny coolies, nearly nude, and bending beneath the weight of bales and boxes, were pushing along in the crowd. In the middle of the road was a gentleman uncomfortably doubled up in a sedan or "norimon," carried by bearers. These are some of the sights and sounds we noticed in our stroll along the streets. A singular feature, we remarked, consisted in huge drums placed at intervals on gaily-decorated stands. As the "many-headed" passed along, some lively member would perform an impromptu solo on this noisy instrument, to the accompaniment of a laughing chorus.

Following in the wake of the throng, we at length arrived at the entrance of a clean broad avenue, flanked by splendid trees, and with handsome granite candelabra-like lamp-posts between them. On an elevated basement at the end we perceived a temple, with a noble flight of steps leading to the open portals. A lean old man, in a quaint gold cap, was squatting on a platform by the door. To him the captain spoke very politely, for he imagined him to be the high priest, and the old fellow, who was remarkably lively, seemed to take much interest in the captain's sword and spyglass. A roar of laughter from the upturned faces of the close-packed crowd below excited our attention, and Araki explained that the old man with the gilded cap was but the beater of the wooden drum which summoned the faithful citizens of Tomo to their prayers.

We entered the temple, and as we stood before the altar we missed the mild, benevolent form of Buddha, which we were accustomed to see gilded and of colossal size. We beheld instead, however, placed aloft, a monstrous horrid mask with goggle-eyes, a pendulous red nose, and a hideous grinning mouth. On either side of this mysterious ogre-like face were female masks, with regular and pleasing features. Araki, a proud man, and a sceptic, threw down a few coins and strode out, apparently somewhat ashamed of his fellow-countrymen's absurd idolatry.

After leaving the sacred fane we proceeded to a pleasant suburb, where we rested in a famous tea-house, perched on a rocky angle which commands a splendid view of the calm blue waters of the Bingo-Nada. Like all these favourite places of resort, this tea-house was a light and elegant structure, with a terrace in front, and charming gardens all around. A priest was kind enough to invite us into his dwelling, where we were indulged with the sight of two dancing girls, famous for their beauty and alluring manners. The description by Captain Saris, of the women of Japan, written in 1613, accurately describes these Eastern Aspasias as they are at the present day. "They were attired in gownes of silke, clapt the one skirt over the other, and so girt to them; bare-legged, only a paire of half buskins bound with silke about their instep; their haire very blacke, and very long, tyed up in a knot upon the crowne in a comely manner, their heads nowhere shaven as the men's were. They were well-faced, handed and footed, cleare skind and white, but wanting colour, which they amend by arte. Of stature low, but very fat, very courteous in behaviour, not ignorant of the respect to be given unto persons according to their fashion."

It is, I am aware, treading on delicate ground, to enter the boudoir and watch the toilet of a lady, and still more dangerous to criticise the fashion, colour, and material of her dress; but as no "Le Follet" is published in Yeddo, to which I can refer my fair readers, I must even risk the imputation of a curiosity which cost an "Actæon" of other days his life!

In the seclusion of her scrupulously clean but simply furnished apartment sits the Niphon belle, in that attitude peculiar to all classes in Japan, her legs bent under her, and the palms of her hands resting on her knees. One of her attendants kneels behind her, and combs her long hair from her forehead, and arranges it in heavy coils upon the top of her head. Great pins of glass, ivory, or tortoiseshell are now placed at oblique angles, and perhaps a bit of scarlet ribbon is added, giving her head a peculiarly piquant, quaint, and picturesque character. The tortoiseshell and golden combs, the enormous chignons worn by European ladies, and the long stiletto hair-pins still affected by the Roman contadina, are not a whit more extravagant than are the ornaments of a Japanese lady's coiffure. The wives of the Mikado are, I believe, the only ladies in Japan who wear their hair hanging loose about their shoulders.

The pattern of our maiden's silken robes is neat, usually finely checkered, and the colours are quiet and unexceptionable. Her ample outer garment has loose hanging sleeves, and her under robe is a very narrow skirt. These two vestments are fastened with a wide sash of most voluminous proportions, which is tied behind in a huge knot. In the tea-gardens this is a very becoming feature in the pretty waitresses, who, bending on one knee, offer you tea and sweetmeats on a lacquered tray. Unlike the ladies of the Flowery Land, our damsel of the Land of the Rising Sun wears no spacious pantaloons, and her feet are bare. Her face is made beautiful by cosmetics, her complexion is whitened with pearl-powder prepared from the dried fruit of the Marvel of Peru, and her lips are painted with a rich vermilion dye.

The ugly fashion of staining the teeth black, and plucking out the hair of the eyebrows, is not followed by our charming "Moosmi," for she remains at present "in maiden meditation fancy free." This unbecoming custom, I quite agree with Mr. Oliphant, appears to be a heartless device of jealous husbands, who wish to keep entirely to themselves a useful household manager to mind their domestic concerns, while they themselves pay visits to the tea-houses, and are waited on by smiling Hebes! I constantly saw among the upturned female faces smiling at the foreigner, many married women, with their hands before their mouths, endeavouring to conceal what they evidently regard as a disfigurement of their features.

A Japanese lady in walking attire forms a rather pretty picture, as, shading her eyes with her open fan, she slides along in her grass-woven sandals, her hair tastefully arranged, and her loose-sleeved jacket partially covering her narrow skirt. I think she contrasts not unfavourably with an English girl in bright-coloured walking dress, and head of portentous size, stepping mincingly along with the celebrated "Grecian bend!"

But when I observe a lady of Niphon on horseback, taking the air, bestriding a high conical wooden saddle, holding on to it in front with both her hands, and her knees up to her elbows, while a barelegged groom leads her sorry nag, I think she presents a figure at once inelegant and absurd; contrasting very unfavourably with a bonny English maiden in a dark riding-habit, which sets off her slender supple form as she sits with easy grace her beautiful Arab mare!

A wealthy man of Tomo, our guide through the town, now invited us to his house. The rooms were bare of furniture, but exquisitely neat and clean. The floors were covered with soft thick mats, and the open windows looked out into trim little gardens abounding in rockwork, ponds of gold-fish, dwarf trees of fantastic shapes, and some magnificent Japanese lilies in full bloom. His wife entered with grapes and slices of melon, and his daughter followed with pipes and tobacco, which she offered on her knee to the unlooked-for visitors. As Araki gave them our history, both matron and maid regarded us with looks of lively interest, and, judging from their "nods and becks, and wreathed smiles," were well pleased with our appearance.

On bidding farewell to our kind entertainers, we wended our way through streets and lanes lined with silent orderly spectators, to the famous saki distilleries, where we passed along dark narrow galleries, full of huge wooden casks and puncheons, and piled with flasks, jars, and queer-shaped vessels filled with the favourite spirit.

It was a source of great amusement to me during our stay at Yokohama, where we remained a short time, to rummage among the art treasures in the bazaars and curiosity shops. The love of the grotesque, so strongly developed among the people, is shown in many ways, and among others in those small wood and ivory carvings called "buttons," which the better classes wear attached to their tobacco-pouches. These exquisite carvings in ivory are difficult to obtain, although inferior imitations are not uncommon.

In the course of my researches I became acquainted with an old curiosity dealer, a melancholy, ugly being, by the way, between whom and myself a close friendship was cemented, in consequence of our common appreciation of these quaint little "curios." He would draw in his breath, and heave a sigh of profound admiration as he produced from some mysterious corner of his shop a figure more elaborately carved or more humorous than usual, which he placed in my hand with a confident air, as if to say "Is it not a choice one?"

I either purchased from himself, or became through his intervention the fortunate possessor of many specimens of these charming gems of art, which are not always procurable for "boos." Some of them are mythical monsters, with obese forms, and loose rolling balls in their capacious mouths; or contorted writhing dragons, with scaly trunks and heads, which could have been suggested only by the remembrance of some hideous dream. Natural objects, however, are very carefully copied. I have a group of toadstools with the stem and gills exactly as in nature, and a melon with the netted roughness peculiar to the rind of that fruit most skilfully imitated. A snake which, with head erect, eyes glistening, and tongue protruding, has eaten his way through the melon, is carved with minute accuracy, even to the rendering of the small curved teeth. I have a very neat figure of a

Musina,* a pretty fox-like animal with a bushy tail, of which the Japanese make great pets. She is represented going off to market, standing on her hind legs, with an aquatic plant to protect her head, while she holds another smaller leaf as a fan. On her arm is slung a gourd to serve as a water-bottle, should she be thirsty on her way. The creature's fur in this ivory gem is wonderfully rendered, and the veins of the leaves are sculptured with the most minute accuracy. The eyes are black and sparkling, and a quaint business-like air is given to the serious face. Although at first sight top-heavy, the artist has so accurately balanced his work, that the little animal stands readily upon its hind feet.

I likewise discovered in my explorations, cameos of grinning faces, carved in low relief on the sides of walnuts, and a charming little bit of carving in solid tortoiseshell, obtained from the nails of the great elephant-footed tortoise. I became possessed also of a female figure balancing a huge water-pot on her head, and a warrior with a terrible counte-

* See Vignette.

nance, who, having overcome his enemy, is placing his foot upon the head of his prostrate foe. He, poor wretch, clenching his fist with rage, and with distorted features, glares with open mouth and wide staring eyes from beneath the shelter of his hat.

In these clever carvings, scenes from daily life are reproduced with marvellous fidelity and effect. In one of my specimens, two small boys are playing at "chequers." One fixes his eyes with a look of anxiety on his *vis-à-vis*, who is about to throw for first move. The other, confident of success, assumes a well-pleased air, though he is obliged to use both hands to hold up the dice box, which is nearly as big as his head. On examining the interior of the dice box, a single die is seen loose within, having all the dots from ace to seize marked with minute accuracy.

Another figure of very skilful workmanship, one of my choicest examples, represents an old man with a beaming countenance, digging with a mattock into a heap of money, which the sharp nose of his dog has discovered for him. His eager attitude is very expressively rendered, and the carving of his dress is as perfect as it can be—the texture and pattern of his garments being accurately copied from the living model, even to the grass sandals on his feet, and the few decayed teeth in the old man's open mouth. On examining the under surface of the money heap, the different coins of Japan—boo, tempo, cash, and cobang—each with its own distinctive marks, are found to be faithfully engraved. The finish of this figure is exquisite.

The impression made on our minds by the people of Japan is, that they are a very paradoxical race. They bow down before and worship the most hideous idols, grovelling in the lowest form of Paganism, or they rise to the contemplation of the sublimest truths of philosophy. They have two kings and two languages. Their great men wear two swords. They live in picturesque and beautiful islands, cultivated to the highest perfection. They plant noble avenues of cedars, and build magnificent temples. As a rule, they are simple and chivalrous in their lives, and their reverence for the dead is great and enduring. They delight in flower-gardens, and their love of natural scenery amounts almost to a passion.

Instead of shoeing their horses with iron, they protect their hoofs with sandals of straw. They do not engrave their crests upon their plate, or stamp them on their envelopes, but bear them about on the back of their outer garment. The keys of their locks are turned in a direction opposite to ours. Their courtiers, instead of donning knee-breeches like our own, trail the lengthened legs of their trowsers more than a yard upon the ground. Their nobles, when disgraced, rip themselves up, and their delinquent priests do penance with their heads concealed in huge bee-hive hats. They wrap up their noses in the cold season, and walk bare-headed in the streets. They tattoo their nude bodies, and almost dispense with clothing, or deck themselves out in most preposterous habiliments. Such is their ingenuity, that they can dwarf trees and variegate leaves, can cause gold-fish to flourish a double tail, can produce at demand pigeons of any pattern of plumage and poodles with hardly any noses, worth mentioning, rear bantams of the smallest dimensions, and cultivate the tallest of chrysanthemums.

But the time had come for our departure, and having weighed anchor, we entered the Suwo-Nada, which is the largest division of the Inland Sea, being nearly sixty miles in length. On the one hand, our eyes rested with pleasure on the lovely shores of Niphon; and on the other, on the fine island of Yasima, which was spread out before us.

We all of us had heard of Scylla and Charybdis, and of that terrible Maelström on the coast of Norway; and some of us, perhaps, had read, with feelings of terror, Edgar Poe's fearful narrative of the ship gradually engulphed in the vortex of the Great Whirlpool; but here, immediately before us, is the famous "Naruto," or Whirlpool of Japan. It is not, however, strictly a whirlpool, "Naruto" meaning "Gate of the Sea, which makes a great noise." It is rather a narrow and winding channel, bounded by dangerous rocks, and through which the waters of the Inland Sea rush with a turbulent impetuosity.

My friend Captain Bullock resolved to shoot the rapids, and take soundings, in the steam tender of the "Actæon." With knowledge and science, her captain piloted her in safety through the dangerous passage. The little craft boldly plunged into the seething waters, the foaming waves rolling onwards, and striving to dash her on the rocks; but the "Dove," undaunted, pursued her steady course, and dropped anchor in the peaceful waters beyond the reefs of Koura. During the passage some junks were seen to be turned round and round many times by the whirls and eddies where the converging currents met.

Trading or other craft are never supposed to venture this way, the families of the rash owners of junks, dashed to pieces on these rocks, being excluded from the benefit of the relief afforded by the Japanese Government to the sufferers in ordinary cases of shipwreck.

CHAPTER XXI.

Simidsu Excursionists—Quack-Doctors—Natural Curiosities—Habits of the Musina—Ursa Major and Minor—Women hauling the Seine—Prolific Life—Village Store—Mode of catching Whales—Japanese Mammals—Madrepores and Mollusca—Shell-Sand—Araki—Sun- and-Moon Shell.

WHEN the "Actæon" dropped anchor in Simidsu, or the "Harbour of Sweet Waters," there was great excitement in the village up the river from which the harbour derives its poetic name. The advent of the vessel was held to be a legitimate occasion for the pleasure-seeking inhabitants to proclaim a general holiday. The bay soon swarmed with pic-nic parties, and the ship was surrounded by a flotilla of boats. The noise and confusion along-side was a babel of distraction. As usual, the women were wildly excited, their chatterings mingling shrilly with the vociferations of the men. Mothers held aloft their infants to obtain a better view. Gaping wonder was depicted in the upturned faces in the boats, and, on all sides, loud clickings of the tongue and mute signs of approval were every instant interchanged.

A motley group soon thronged the decks, all dressed in their best, the women and girls barefooted, but with their hair neatly arranged. The men and boys often bore on their wrists tame falcons, and little nuthatches in tall wicker-cages. Quack-doctors were especially numerous and important; and the O-Esha, or chief doctor of the ship, found favour in their eyes. "A fellow-feeling makes us wondrous kind."

One ancient empiric paused abruptly before me, feeling his pulse, lolling out his tongue, and complacently patting his stomach. That pantomime having been duly enacted, he next proceeded with great gravity to swallow one of his own pills, and went away with a well-satisfied smile at his own performance.

The people of Japan are fond of natural curiosities, although the mythic element is not so strongly developed in them on this point as it is with the Chinese. Their monsters are equally as quaint, but are never so astounding in their proportions, or so grotesque in their hideousness, as the terrible dragons, unicorns, and phœnixes you see painted on the inside of the screens facing the Yahmuns, or public buildings, of China.

Our visitors brought off for sale the knotty wens of trees; snake-gourds as tall as a man, and no thicker than a cucumber; strange plants, with mottled leaves; cowrie shells; branches of coral; and even toads and rats, in small square cages, were offered to us by those who were anxious to dispose of them.

In the names which the Chinese give to animals, the poetic nature of their language, and their fondness for simile, are strongly indicated. Among them the cat is a "household fox;" the bat becomes the "heavenly rat;" the porpoise is the "river pig;" while, strange to say, the scaly ant-eater is the "hill-carp," and is said to be the "only fish that has legs." Some of the Japanese names of animals are, however, very appropriate; anakuma, for example, or "hole-bear," is the appellation by which the badger is known.

Some of the objects brought on board by the quack-doctors were sufficiently curious, and suggested reminiscences of the earlier ages of medicine in England. One offered leeches in an earthen jar; another displayed a bloated toad; a third paraded frogs, skinned, dried, and spitted on bamboo skewers; and a fourth was the fortunate possessor of a bundle of dried vipers, with the jaws extended to show their poison-fangs. Others had snails packed up in grass, or bamboo-boxes crammed with slugs, heads of the singular fish Fistularia, or flute-mouth, the velvet-covered budding horns of deer, dried camomile flowers, and fern-powder.

One of the prettiest things I procured from the good people of Simidsu was a Musina, or female Tanuki, the head of which was revealed to me softly nestling on the breast of a young boy. I purchased her, and she soon became a great pet, not only of her master, but of all on board. I brought her with me as far as the Cape, when, to my disappointment, she became sick and died.

The Japanese are very fond of this little animal. Old Kæmpfer describes it in a few words: "Tanuki is a very singular kind of an animal, of a brownish dark colour, with a snout not unlike a fox's snout, and pretty small." My playful little Musina was very much like a racoon. When she was hungry and in quest of food, she ran like a fox, tail on end, sniffing the ground with her inquisitive sharp nose. Like Reynard, alas! she was also too fond of poultry, and got into sad disgrace by killing the captain's bantams and pheasants. She was partial also to raw eggs, which she cleverly held between her fore-feet; cracking them across, and, as the two halves fell apart, licking out the contents with her tongue. Musina at times was very petulant. She became enraged at the sound of the drum beating to quarters, and would shake with fury any piece of cloth of a red colour. At Simidsu, the people profess to believe that the Tanuki lives only in the crater of their beloved mountain, the peerless Fusiyama.

I procured likewise a very fierce little creature, allied in nature and habits to the weasels, but very like a tiny otter in appearance. The Japanese call it Itatsi. It is a species of Vison, one of the genera of Mustelidæ. In Kœmpfer's history it is very briefly alluded to. "The Itutz," he says, "is a small animal, of a reddish colour." When angry it makes a hissing sound, like a brood of young owls or hawks. The Japanese encourage the Itatsi to take up its abode in the roofs of their houses, in order to keep in check the rats and other vermin, upon which it principally subsists. The one I had killed a rat, with which I presented it, in an instant.

Our two Japanese bears were a source of much amusement to the sailors. They roamed at large about the ship, and were very docile, but their motto seemed to be "Noli me tangere;" for when teased they would bite their tormentor severely. They had been christened Ursa Major and Ursa Minor, the former being the favourite. Major was more wilful and mischievous than Minor, and more frequently in hot water. He was not averse to poultry, and would boldly abstract fowls from a Japanese covered basket left for a moment in his way. He once escaped with one screaming bird in each paw, was forthwith pursued, and, not without an indignant protest, was made to relinquish his prey. On another occasion, seizing his opportunity, he clawed a favourite bantam out of his coop, and immediately consumed it on the spot. He would walk down the accommodation-ladder, enter a canoe alongside, and seize an albicore nearly as big as himself. He once jumped overboard, and swam to some native boats lying off the ship, into one of which he climbed, to the consternation of the old women in possession, who held up boards behind which they hid themselves in terror. He was brought on board and tied up for his bad behaviour, not, however, without remonstrances and cries in a peevish voice, like that of a cross boy exclaiming, "Don't! don't!" He was partial to sweets, and when the mouth of a jam-pot with which he was presented proved too small for him, he seized hold of the coxswain's hand, and made of it a cat's paw to abstract the tempting contents. He had rum and sugar given him by a "monkey" of a boy as mischievous as himself. He partook of it, and soon became very intoxicated, staggering about the deck, and finally falling to the ground insensible. With careful treatment, however, he was restored, even after his life had been despaired of. On one occasion he disappeared. He was supposed to have fallen overboard, or to have swum ashore. His description was made out, and a reward offered for his recovery by the police. Next day he was found fast asleep in the hammock-netting, and resumed his mischievous pranks, in perfect ignorance of the trouble and anxiety he had caused his friends.

On the east coast of Niphon, and not far from Tatiyama, are two small islets, named Takano-Sima and Okino-Sima. We were prohibited from rambling on the mainland, for it belonged to a Daimio unfriendly to foreigners; but the two little islets were placed at our disposal for the purpose of exercise and recreation during our stay at this anchorage. Here, undisturbed, I was enabled to watch the habits of many molluscous creatures, for my observatories were exposed to the rolling waves of the Pacific, and had not been disturbed, except by fishermen, for ages. The narrow beach was fringed by a low brushwood, in which the white, umbellate flowers of Crinum asiaticum were conspicuous, while the interior of the islets was occupied by huge fig-trees (Ficus nitida), which, with firs and larches, form dark shady labyrinths, the chosen abode of Helix simodæ and a little Bulimulus. The proliferous fronds of the handsome fern Woodwardia japonica sprang in profusion from the humid soil, and the trunks of the Coniferæ were green with Drymoglossum, a curious fern with narrow fertile fronds growing erect from slender, twisted stems. Here, in the calm, warm days, came fishermen to haul the seine, and boatloads of women followed from the mainland to assist their husbands. The song and merry laughter of the women hauling at the rope, and the noise and splashing of the men in the water, mingled with the loud cawing of the rooks in the great fig-trees, produced on the mind a novel and pleasing impression. As the seine came slowly in, we used to notice, besides goodly fish of the larger sort, cow-fishes and sea-scorpions, squids, cuttles, file-fishes, and long-clawed flat-legged swimming crabs. Crawling on the rocks between tide marks, where the boulders are covered with soft green seaweed, or hiding in the fissures and furrows, were numbers of Peronia Tongana, looking like shell-less Chitons and veritable Pulmonifers living in the sea!

Not far from Tatiyama is a snug little harbour called Tago, in which are numerous small coves, where one may escape from the prying inquisitiveness of the people and collect specimens in peace. In all these small bays, sandstone rocks, clothed with stunted oaks and dwarf firs, rise abruptly from the shingle of the beach, and a few miles inland are green hills which tower up all around. Against the water-worn rocks on the beach are loose rounded stones, heaped up by the efforts of the ever restless tide. The yellow flowers of Hemerocallis, the red spotted turbans of the tiger-lily, a trailing

Clematis, and a pretty blue Scilla, grow on the shingly soil, while Pitcairnia straminea, Lycopodium lineare, Pteris cretica, and a Dendrobium fill up the fissures of the cliffs. Above high-water mark, but exposed to the saline influence of the tide, adhering to the under surface of the stones, crawling in damp shady corners, or nestling in the weed-grown crannies, are thousands of Realia, small cyclostomatous snails. These are not the only creatures here observed, however, for Lygiæ, or Sea-Woodlice, run out in great excitement, Armidillidia roll themselves up in balls, crickets hop nimbly aside, and sinuous Geophili, harmless centipedes, hastily seek the shelter of the surrounding stones.

The day after our arrival there was great excitement in the village. All Kino-O-Sima was out of doors. A whale was reported in the offing. There was much noise and shouting. A dozen boats were quickly launched, and started off in wild pursuit. Long, gaily-painted, sharp-prowed boats, propelled by four powerful sculls, each worked by two men standing, darted through the water. A smart hand was placed in the bows in charge of the harpoon; while others, eager but still, squatted on the huge black nets coiled up in the boat. The boats soon approached, and quickly surrounded the whale, which they wounded repeatedly with their lances and harpoons; and, when he was exhausted from loss of blood, enclosed him in their strong nets, and hauled him ashore.

The village abreast of the anchorage at Kino-O-Sima is pleasantly situated, and the houses are well arranged in rows, with neat green lanes between, formed of bamboo and other plants. Conspicuous among the houses is the general store, where, as in England, you constantly see little children and women dropping in for the purchase of a pennyworth (or tempo-worth) of treacle, oil, saki, dried fish, string, sugar, or rice.

In the front of the village is a large square space open to the sea. Here, on the beach, are fishing-boats hauled up, long dark nets spread out to dry, noisy rooks feeding on scraps of offal, and picturesque groups of fishers and women.

Anchored off the entrance of the Kino channel, I was very fortunate in obtaining specimens. Time was when a European naturalist, visiting the shores of the great island named Zipangu, as Marco Polo calls it, would have had but a sorry chance of learning anything about the zoology of Japan; but now, with the imperial flag (a red ball on a white ground) at the fore, and Araki, an officer of high rank, on intimate and familiar terms with all on board, we found the people very friendly in their intercourse. Amused and puzzled at my passion for skulls, Araki gave orders to the hunters to provide specimens for me, and in a day or two an antlered deer was brought alongside, and soon became mine by right of purchase. Next followed two fine does, then a badger and a tanuki. A fine old yellow-haired sow also became my property for a consideration of ten "boos," but she illustrated the saying about "a pig in a poke," for though, as she lay on her side on the quarter-deck, she looked a magnificent specimen, alas! she had been speared through the mouth, and her skull was found on examination to be shattered, and consequently worthless, and her lean carcase was quite unfit for food.

Many of the animals brought down for sale were cunningly done up in straw. A living wild-cat thus secured could do no mischief, though she flashed fire from her glaring, angry eyes. In fashion similar a little dead monkey was brought to me, its brown face only visible. It resembled one of those Egyptian mummy-cases in the British Museum, with the face painted on the outside. Two men were seen, on one occasion, trotting along the shore abreast of the ship, bearing something on a pole between them, very much resembling a flayed child. Frightful suspicions of cannibalism flitted across my mind. They stopped, deposited their burden on the beach, and placidly awaited the arrival of our party. A near inspection showed me that the anthropoid creature was a large monkey divested of its skin—trussed in point of fact, and ready for the spit. It was kindly offered by our Japanese Nimrods to supply our gastronomic necessities; for they imagined that all the wild-cats, pigs, and badgers which we purchased or received were boiled in the coppers, and served out as savoury rations to the hungry sailors. Great, therefore, was their astonishment, when friend Bedwell neatly decapitated the quadrumane, leaving the body neglected on the beach, and bearing off the head, carefully wrapped in a newspaper, for the doctor's delectation.

There is one tribe of mollusca which usually escapes the notice of collectors, on account of their living buried in madrepore-masses and corals. As an instance of the facility with which good specimens of these burrowing mollusks may be obtained, I will relate my O-Sima experience.

A shallow bay indents the promontory on the mainland on the opposite side, which, on investigation, offers nothing so tempting as the numbers of huge old madrepores which strew the beach. They are large and heavy, and how to transport them to a convenient spot was a question that required some consideration. Collinson solved the problem, however, by selecting a number of small Nipong children, whose curiosity prompted them to follow us; and allotting a madrepore to each they bore them cheerfully, but in amazement, to the opposite shore, and were rewarded with small coin. One pretty little girl was detected, after the arrival of the others, fraudulently appropriating a madrepore, which she pretended she had brought all the way, and therefore claimed the usual award. On being found out she ran away, discomfited and ashamed, amid the jeers and laughter of her boy-companions.

When the madrepores were brought on board, I had them broken up with a hammer, when the shells fell out, and were carefully collected; in this manner I obtained specimens of Jouannetia globosa, Parapholas quadrizonalis, and Leptoconchus, red-brown boring Lithophagi, gaping Gastrochænæ, besides parasitic Arks and other nestling bivalves.

The vast rolling waves of the Pacific washed the strand, where children and aged crones were seen gathering bits of driftwood and charcoal, and where village curs were equally intent on cast-up offal and the remains of shipwrecked cuttles. Might I not

also claim a share of old Ocean's waifs and strays—
the "jetsam and flotsam" of the grey and melancholy waste? Yes; for in many a sheltered cove
the heaped-up sand was rich in shells, when green,
lengthy ridges of broad-leaved seaweed fringed the
outline of the bay. Here were sea-hares and bubble-shells, odd-fashioned crabs and tiny fragile shrimps.
Some of these had lived their little day in the
shallow pools hard by, but most of the more
beautiful forms had been brought hither by the
Kuro-Sino, or Japan-stream, which sweeps along
the outer or eastern shores of the Japanese islands.
This Pacific gulf-stream runs at the rate of seventy
miles a day, bearing along on its bosom floating
islets of Sargossa weed, and many animal forms
of oceanic origin, such as Clio and Cavolina,
glass-like Pteropods; the transparent shells of
Spirialis and Atlanta; and those Pelagian skeleton-shrimps, Alima and Erichthus. Besides these
I found the hemispherical pearly eyes of oceanic
cuttles, the round bladdery floats of the gulf-weed,
and the carapaces of the sailor-crab called Planes.

Many other forms, alas! I also saw, but was unable to identify; exquisite organisms only indicated by stray fragments and detached members, the minute anatomy of which was very elaborate. How the fragile shells of Bulla, which were somewhat numerous, had escaped destruction from the rolling stones among which they lay, was to me a mystery, although I easily imagined their safety ensured from the buffetings of the waves by reason of their lightness. From the same cause the shells of Ianthina were cast ashore here in a perfect condition. As for the milk-white wentletraps and polished Eulimæ, and the tribe of tiny Rissoids which I likewise disentombed, they were once living inhabitants of the giant Laminariæ that now lay rotting on the beach. The Foraminifera or Rhizopods were very abundant in some portions of this marine *débris*, and as the eye alighted upon their highly sculptured forms, when scanning under the lens this mass of crude fragments, I was quite startled to see the contrast between the rude inorganic bodies and the perfect results of animal life.

The contemplation of so much beauty in so small a space, of so many organic gems in a little *débris*, could not but fill the mind with wonder! "Every wisp and every wrinkle of the grand nebula of Orion," says Professor Nicholl, "is a sand-heap of stars." My sand-heap here, though of less proportions, was equally as wonderful.

*   *   *   *   *

Three Japanese gentlemen, who messed with us for some months, rendered our stay at Kino-O-Sima extremely pleasant, and the people belonging to the villages were very friendly in their intercourse. Araki, a Japanese officer of high rank, was a tall handsome man, with prominent features, very much resembling those of a North American Indian; he was always very abstemious, dressed elegantly, and was courtly in his manner.

Kuro-Sima, the next in rank, was an oldish large-headed man, short of stature, and somewhat grotesque in appearance. He was very jocular, and had no objection to creature comforts, which he evidently enjoyed.

Tatish, the interpreter, was a wily, spare, little, pock-marked man, with a sinister eye. He possessed great sagacity and cunning, was proud of his knowledge of English, and always a little afraid of Araki; being, in fact, concerned about the safety of his head especially, after a night of saki and conversation, when he feared he might, perhaps, have been too communicative concerning Japanese manners and customs.

The native pilot was a cheery old man, with a cautious, wrinkled, brown face. His weather-beaten head was tied up in an old blue handkerchief, and his gaunt form was nearly always bent in the most obsequious manner.

One of the most beautiful of the bivalve shells of Japan is the Amussium Japonicum, a kind of large smooth Scallop. The Japanese fishermen call it "Tsuki-hi-kai," or "Sun-and-moon shell," from its presenting a yellow disk on one side, and a white one on the other. Many shells have native names, which are known only to the fishermen. On my inquiring of Araki the name of a shell, he would call one of the boatmen, and ask him, saying with a smile, Japanese words were too numerous, and his head too small to contain them all.

Seeing the interest I took in objects of natural history, he kindly communicated my wants to the fishermen of Tatiyama. The collecting, however, of these poor but willing hands was too indiscriminating. They brought off large basketsful of broken, wave-worn shells from the beach, most of them more like each other than anything else. In consequence, when darkness veiled the ungracious act, they were quietly passed over the ship's side, and the waters of their native bay closed over them for ever.

CHAPTER XXII.

The Literature of Japan—Books—Illustrations—Voyage Home—Oceanic Phenomena—Black Fish—Bonitoes—Dolphins—Floating Tree—Pelagian Molluscs—Sea Nettles—Skeleton Shrimps—Sailor Crabs—Rapid Growth of Barnacles—A Pretty Kettle of Fish.

ALTHOUGH I am not acquainted with the literature of Japan, which, I am informed, is rather extensive, I cannot conclude my observations on this interesting country without making a few remarks upon it. In the houses of the wealthy may be seen many books and maps. Their works on geography contain accounts of their thousand and one islands; their dramas are of a sensational character; they delight in long poems on love and war, and have abundance of memoirs, legends, books on etiquette, and descriptions of their ceremonies, manners, and customs. They have even, I am informed, a national encyclopædia. Many of these works are profusely illustrated by woodcuts and engravings printed in colours. I possess myself what I believe to be a rare little book, consisting of a series of beautiful etchings of towns and scenery, done on copper.

Among my Japanese books, two are very excellent. One is a book of birds, reminding me somewhat of the splendid "Birds of Australia," in which Gould, assisted by his wife, has given us drawings not only of the birds themselves, but also of the flowers, plants, trees, or localities which are most affected by them. This work is something of the same nature. The Japanese artist has depicted the swallows winging their way through the air, the familiar wren hopping jauntily about the flowers in the garden, the snow-bunting perched on the branches of snow-laden fir-trees, the sportive fly-catchers pursuing their insect prey in the bright sun, the butcher-bird sitting watchful, with cruel eye, on the outstretched arm of an oak, the little lively tits peering about for grubs among the branches of Persimmon trees, the coot dreaming on the margin of a lake, the lark walking on the ground, the sparrow in the rice-field, the plover rising from the swamp, the pigeon sitting quiet in a mulberry tree, the egret stalking among the iris leaves, and the kingfisher perched on the top of an upright stump, looking down upon the water.

Another very interesting book in my collection is an illustrated edition of the "Wonders of Nature and Art in Japan." It contains a view of a burning mountain in a state of eruption, probably that of Ohæsima, pouring out a volume of smoke, stones, and lava from its crater. There is a capitally painted view of a mine, probably a gold mine in the island of Sado, where, by the light of oil lamps suspended from the sides, the miners are seen descending the dark shafts by means of nearly perpendicular notched trees, till they reach the recesses and cavities in the dim region below, which is occupied by other workers, whom we see crouching on stages and mats using the pick, and diligently searching for the precious ore. Another drawing represents some celebrated waterfall, which, forming a succession of cascades, dashes down the cedar-crowned heights of a steep and rocky mountain, with the rosy clouds of sunset floating around its base. A wonderful observatory, supported by vertical slender piles, is perched on the very apex of a lofty sugar-loaf hill. A covered staircase reaches to the aërial house, by which the almost perpendicular sides of the mountain peak can be ascended. Here a long and narrow bridge seems to cross an arm of the sea, and there are many other drawings depicting the natural appearance of the country; a wild cavern-scene, for instance, of rugged rocks and foaming water; a representation of some gigantic conifer, cedar, or fir tree, the girth of which a party at the base are endeavouring to measure by joining hands. In one picture, a group of excited beings is seen struggling with the strings of a gigantic kite, on which a fearful dragon is painted, while clouds of coloured paper descend from it. In a drawing which represents several enormous fir-trees, very ancient and contorted, men with burdens on their backs are seen passing under the arching roots which rise above the surface of the ground, to indicate their huge dimensions. The famous Naruto, or whirlpool in the Inland Sea, is depicted, with its rocky dangers and eddying waters. The artist has even attempted to realise the fearful earthquake wave, similar to that which, not very long ago, overwhelmed the town of Simoda. The perils of whaling form the subjects of some startling pictures. The boatmen are hurling spears from their painted boats, and the dark leviathan of the deep is seen plunging beneath the foaming waters, his mighty tail being the principal object in the foreground of the picture.

Tea-houses, embowered in clouds of the pink-coloured blossoms of the almond tree, and overlooking a river on which boats are sailing, and distant hills; bridges of vast proportions, with complicated wooden beams, put together with consummate skill and ingenuity; a snow storm; a long, low, undulating bridge, like the uneven back of the far-famed sea-serpent, are also among the wonders of nature and art contained in this curious Japanese volume.

* * * * *

Our voyage home was not distinguished by any event demanding particular notice. The capture of a recent species of Belerophina, a form imagined to be only found in a fossil state, and the representative of those great extinct cephalopods which formerly disported themselves on the surface of primæval seas, is, however, worthy of record. During the monotony of long tedious voyages, even trivial objects are often invested with a strange fictitious interest; the otherwise unoccupied mind finding a dreamy pleasure in contemplating the few oceanic phenomena which present themselves. The vigorous leap of the bonitoes, and the glittering bodies of the flying-fish, as they drop exhausted one after the other into the sea; the huge rolling bodies of unwieldy black-fish, their dark skins rough with barnacles, moving through the water; the pretty white boatswain-bird, with his marline-spike of a tail, hovering round the glittering vane at the mainmast head; the azure glint of the dolphins shining through the deep pellucid water; a passing ship; the capture of a shark; a patch of floating gulf-weed, with its colony of sailor-crabs and little fishes; the spar of some lost ship, white with clustering barnacles; the clouds, the water-spouts, the changes of the wind, are all so many incidents which are viewed and watched with absorbing interest.

About one hundred miles from Java Head, at a time when the sea was nearly calm, a huge tree, torn by some tempest from its native forest, came drifting by the ship, hoary with clustering Lepades, and with swimming-crabs clinging to it as shipwrecked mariners to a raft. Eager for the barnacles, short, banded trunk-fish kept close alongside, making sudden onslaughts upon the helpless cirrhepedes. A shoal of bright green parrot-fish hovered in the rear, and more lustrous still, three blue sharks were darting about. In the distance, a school of brown cetaceans, round-backed and long-nosed, came coursing along, vaulting, head downwards, and wantonly pursuing each other. Onwards they went, by fifties and by hundreds, leaping, tumbling, and dashing the spray about, so as to cause the mast-headman to sing out from aloft, "Something like breakers on the starboard bow." The whole surface of the water was alive with those fragile lesser forms of being which constitute of themselves a peculiar Pelagian faunula. Among these might be observed the blue vesicles of Physalia and the indigo disks of Porpita, the pellucid bells and globes and mushroom bodies of the Acalepha, or Sea-nettles, and the glassy shrimps, Erichthus and Alima. When, by means of a towing net, these were assembled together in a vessel of sea-water, the interest was doubled, for now we began to discern the erratic evolutions of the Entomostraca, the steady progress of the small cerulean Pontia, and the skeleton-form of long-eyed Leucifer. These moved almost invisible among the equally pellucid Sagittæ, true arrows, darting, as their name implies, with rigid bodies through the water. Then uprose with flapping wings the globose Cavolina, and Styliola in her tube-like shell. Amid these varied examples of oceanic life, what is that tiny floating bubble? It is nautiloid, and yet no nautilus, nor is there any keel to constitute it an Atlanta—it is a recent Belerophina!

Although it is perfectly true of the large-headed transparent shrimps comprising the family Phronomidæ that they are more or less parasitic, being found stowed away in the pouches and other cavities of the equally pellucid Acalephæ, yet sometimes they swim freely about, and are frequently taken in the towing-net. I have obtained a specimen from the cavity of a large Salpa, and they may, therefore, be said to be parasitic on mollusca as well as on Acalepha. In its free and independent state, when observed in a vessel of seawater, Phronima atlantica is perfectly transparent, and the slender arms and tumid hands are covered with red-brown dots. In its habits it is somewhat peculiar, even for a shrimp. Suspended head downwards in the water, it remains motionless like a spider in its web, the long hind legs extended with the tarsal joints all bent back, the prehensile arms, with their gibbose spotted hands, arched inwards, and the tail curved forward towards the head. In this attitude of attention it remains eagerly on the watch, and while staring with its great eyes, separating its jaws, and keeping ready its mandibles, the false feet of the abdomen are incessantly at work producing a current towards the mouth. No sooner is some minute organic particle drawn within the influence of the vortex than the head and tail of the Phronima are brought together, and the object is immediately seized, and, if large enough, conveyed by the thumb and finger of the freckled hands to the mouth and greedily devoured. When placed in spirits the skin becomes opaque, the colour of the legs is changed into a pale yellow, and the red-brown spots disappear. When we compare the delicate oceanic organisms, seen fresh from the deep sea, with the specimens in our bottles, well may we mournfully exclaim with St. Pierre, "Our books are but the romance of nature, and our museums her tombs."

At Ascension, while the ship's company were fishing from the maindeck ports, some excitement was occasioned by one of their hooks being seized apparently by a large fish. The imaginary prize was heavy, and when rapidly hauled up, appeared to the amused bystanders in the form of an old iron tea-kettle without a spout! Curiosity induced a sailor to peer into the interior, when he observed two eyes of some strange animal, undreamed of in his philosophy, gazing at him. Attempts were made to get him out, but the occupant could not be dislodged. Here was a pretty kettle of fish! As persuasion was of no avail, a bold hand was introduced, when it was immediately seized by a fleshy coil, and retained by a hundred suckers. The hand was forcibly withdrawn in terror, while the great eyes continued to stare upwards from the place of security where it had settled itself. The kettle with its mysterious lodger was now submitted to the doctor, who was expected to solve all questions respecting this strange phenomenon. While pondering on the best means of dislodging the creature, he unexpectedly relieved us from the dilemma by suddenly making his exit, and shuffling rapidly along the deck in a grotesque and startling manner, revealing at the same time the form and action of a great warty cuttle-fish. Alas! poor Octopus rugosus! He was at once caught, and very soon became a specimen in spirits.

THE END.

www.ingramcontent.com/pod-product-compliance
Lightning Source LLC
Chambersburg PA
CBHW032049220426
43664CB00008B/932